About the Author

Beginning as a young construction worker in Cuba, Pedro Ross became a teacher during Cuba's great literacy campaigns of the 1960s, and served three terms as General Secretary of Cuba's labor federation, the CTC (The Workers' Central Union of Cuba)—and in that capacity developed a nationwide series of "Labor Parliaments" dedicated to some form of resolution to the economic collapse. Upon retirement, he was appointed Ambassador to Angola, a post he held for several years. Now in his eighties, he is still active in Cuba's ongoing revolution.

HOW THE WORKERS' PARLIAMENT SAVED THE CUBAN REVOLUTION

Reinvigorating Resistance and Struggle after the Collapse of the Soviet Union

PEDRO ROSS LEAL

MONTHLY REVIEW PRESS

New York

Copyright © 2022 by Monthly Review Press
All Rights Reserved

Library of Congress Cataloging-in-Publication Data
available from the publisher.

ISBN paper: 978-1-58367-978-4
ISBN cloth: 978-1-58367-979-1

Typeset in Bulmer MT Std

MONTHLY REVIEW PRESS, NEW YORK
monthlyreview.org

5 4 3 2 1

Contents

Foreword by Chris Remington | 9

PART ONE | 17
A Brief Introduction | 19
Why Workers' Parliaments? | 23
Fidel Saw It Coming | 26
A Congress in Military Uniforms | 27
What Is a Special Period in Peacetime? | 27
The Fourth Party Congress and the Start of the Special Period | 28
Measures to Address the Crisis | 30
Enemy Encouragement of Social Indiscipline and Vandalism | 30
Fidel Meets the People | 31
The People Respond | 32
"It Is Easier to Find a Dinosaur Crossing the Street Than
    a Pumpkin in the Market" | 33
It Was Not the First Time | 34
"Yes, We Can" | 35
Why Do Unions Exist? | 36
Analysis, Measures, Actions | 37
The Second Ordinary Session of the National Assembly
    of People's Power | 38
What the Workers Say in the Parliaments | 40
Fidel Reflects, Argues, Gives His Opinion, Promotes Discussion | 41
People Work Because They Must | 43
"We Haven't Always Done Things Right by Consulting" | 44
The Sources of the Black Market | 45
Our Proposal | 46
Workers' Assemblies into Workers' Parliaments | 47
The Call | 50

The Preparation | 50
The Workers Are the Owners | 52
A Light at the End of the Tunnel | 53
Unequivocal Support | 53
Sociopolitical and Opinion Studies: The First Survey | 54
A Vast School of Economics | 55
The Issue of Prices | 55
Reducing Employment Rolls . . . But How? | 56
Our Meeting with the Cigar Workers' Parliament | 58
Keeping Fidel Informed | 60
With the Milkmen in Pinar del Río | 61
Workers' Parliaments in Camagüey | 62
The Workers' Parliament at the Lenin Central Workshop | 63
With Fidel: Salary Guarantee and Other Topics | 66
The Building Contractor Contingents | 67
Exchanging Ideas with Fidel | 69
Another Survey: Workers Endorse the Parliaments | 71
Assessment Time: What Happened in the Parliaments? | 72
A Faint Ray of Light | 75
The Final Summary of the Workers' Parliaments | 77
The Ministry of Finances and Prices Reports | 79
The Debate | 85
The International Solidarity of Trade Unionists | 86
Conclusions | 89

PART TWO | 91
The Nightmare of a Devastating Hurricane | 93
The Origins of Cuban Nationality | 94
A Fecund Truce | 97
Martí's Legacy | 97
The Imperialist Intervention of the United States | 100
The Platt Amendment | 103
The Second Occupation of Cuba by the United States | 105
First Governments of the Neocolonial Republic | 106
The Machado Dictatorship | 107

The September 4 Coup d'état and the 100 Days Government | 109
Historical Significance of the Revolution of 1933 | 111
The 1940 Constitution | 111
Fulgencio Batista: Demagogy and Repression | 113
The Authentic Governments | 114
Eduardo Chibás: Decency versus Money | 116
The Coup of March 10, 1952 | 116
Popular Repudiation Grows | 118
The Assaults of July 26, 1953 | 118
"Condemn Me, It Doesn't Matter, History Will Absolve Me" | 120
The Release of the "Moncadists" | 122
The *Granma* | 122
The November 30 Uprising in Santiago de Cuba | 125
The National Liberation War | 125
The Triumph of the Revolution | 133
Cuba Transforms Itself | 133
Playa Girón (Bay of Pigs) | 135
New Paths | 136
The War Against the Bandits | 137
The United States Tries to Isolate Cuba | 138
The Mongoose Plan | 139
The October Crisis | 139
Cuba Built; the United States Attacked | 141
Transformations of Cuban Economy and Society | 142
Rectifying Errors | 144
The Revolution's Social Initiatives | 145
The Cuban Revolution's Foreign Policy | 147
Epilogue | 150

Appendix A | 156
Bibliography | 160
Notes | 165

Foreword

THIS SLENDER, INTENSE, AND CANDID book by Comrade Pedro Ross Leal, retired General Secretary of the Cuban Workers Unions (CTC—Central de Trabajadores de Cuba) and lifelong communist, having served the Cuban working class and people throughout his entire working life, is essential reading. Essential because it is historically unique, but more importantly because it is a tour de force of working-class power in action. The emphasis is on power: the working class in power sorting out immense challenges as faced by Cuba in the 1990s through to the present day. There is no "magic wand," no savior on a white horse, just reliance on themselves as workers.

The collapse of the USSR (Union of Soviet Socialist Republics) in the early 1990s, the subsequent catastrophic impact on the then Socialist world and workers movement worldwide, the ideologically driven enhanced blockade of Cuba by Ronald Reagan (and subsequent US presidents), placed the survival of the Cuban Revolution in extreme difficulties. Under the direct leadership and initiative of Fidel Castro, the Cuban Commander in Chief, but driven by the trade unions, Labor Parliaments were created in this "Special Period in times of peace," to ensure Cuba's survival.

The Cuban working class, the Cuban people, the trade unions, the Communist Party and other mass organisations found the solutions to the daily crises and blockade that threatened their very existence. It was not a question of repeating slogans from classic and historic Marxist theoreticians. It was not a question of regurgitating readymade solutions from different eras and different countries. It was about exercising raw power in the workplaces, of applying the distilled history of Cuban revolutionary experience over decades to tackling the issues of the day.

Immensely hard and frank discussions in thousands of meetings in a period of just 45 days in Cuban workplaces addressed collapsed production, absenteeism, critical shortages of electricity, water, fuel, spare parts, transport, and housing. In addition there were the questions of redeploying workers in failed enterprises, corruption and the black market, currency reform, preserving national sovereignty and independence, and upholding the core values of the Revolution—Education, Health, Social Equality.

From this intense and massive engagement of over three million workers came the survival strategies would ensure that Cuba emerged from the Special Period. The tactics of the United States to ensure that the blockade (which has never weakened) brought about change by internal subversion and rot was and has been countered by the continued emphasis on the need for clarity of mind and unity amongst the Cuban people. Such clarity and unity will win this struggle of ideas.

In addition to the explanation and demonstration of working class power in action, not shirking from hard decisions and yet never surrendering the power that was established in 1959, also emerges the international solidarity toward Cuba from working people around the world.

Russian, French, Spanish, Japanese, British, Italian, Scandinavian, African, Asian, Latin American, North American and many other trade unionists rallied in their internationalist duty to support Cuba during this period. The duty of every revolutionary is to make revolution at home. To show internationalist support to Cuba (and other Socialist states) is a necessity, not a romantic notion, though sometimes some become confused and forget this. Each and every day a Socialist state survives is another day that imperialism and the forces of reaction lose.

How ideas, combined with organisation and ideological determination, can change events is demonstrated by how British solidarity aid developed in 1997–99. Two British Communists, both UNISON members, sitting in the mountains of the Sierra Maestra, discussed the critical state the Ambrosio Grillo Hospital near Santiago de Cuba which had been reduced to a desperate shell by the blockade. The Ambrosia Grillo Hospital was typical of many in Cuba. It started life in pre-revolutionary times as a tuberculosis hospital. Despite the blockade the health service set up by the Cubans following the Revolution had managed to long since eradicate the disease though it is still prevalent in other countries in the region. These days the hospital remains a large general hospital with six hundred beds, serving a wide catchment area. The hospital had scores of well trained and highly motivated doctors and nurses, but virtually no working equipment and few drugs, all a direct result of the blockade.

The final hour of the visit was to the hospital transport section. Most staff at the Grillo lived in Santiago de Cuba; transport to get the hospital staff to work had been reduced to one, last, overworked and spares-starved bus.

As the hospital was robbed of virtually every necessity from bedding to medicines by the blockade and the damage it inflicted on the people and economy, the Health trade union and the Ministry of Health had worked hard to guarantee the survival of the Grillo. The transport crisis now presented the possibility that the Grillo might be forced to close. If this was to happen it would be the first hospital in the country to be brought down by the blockade. And, to a Cuban, there is no more potent symbol of the progress made since the Revolution, even in the teeth of opposition, than the Americas' most comprehensive health service.

The visitors were asked if there was any way that they could help. Help in this case meant more than a few spares to patch up the virtually unpatchable vehicles. It meant good, working buses.

The visitors and their union colleagues had to ask themselves some searching questions. If working-class solidarity for one of the most courageous small socialist countries in the world meant more than token gestures and lip-service, something bigger was required—bigger thinking and bigger actions.

The thought entered their heads that they might be able to supply a complete bus. Maybe more than one? Maybe with other equipment inside it?

A Cuban health official hinted that it might be possible for Cuba to divert a ship to Britain to collect the shipment.

The British working class, like any army, has its fair share of moaners, armchair generals and naysayers. Some of them sniffed at the idea. Others relished in undermining the idea. To divert a ship would cost $300,000, rather a lot of money for a used bus. The armchair generals for all their talk of solidarity gloated at this stumbling block.

The UNISON workers thought again, only this time bigger not smaller. If a ship was going to be so costly, and a major investment by the Cubans of their hard-earned dollars, it was time to work out what exactly would make that effort worthwhile.

Further discussions with the General Secretary of the CTC (the Cuban TUC), Pedro Ross, helped to clarify the situation. If there were more buses it would help. A lot more buses would be even better. Ambulances would be good, plus serious shipments of medicines. Fire engines are always useful.

The UNISON workers realized that the scale of the venture was as much an obstacle as the challenge itself.

As communists and trade union organizers which they excelled at, putting aside the do-gooder or charity mentality, it was now necessary to apply the organizing skills required to deliver the challenge. Motivating and mobilizing the British working class was the organizing challenge. As much as the solidarity aid would assist Cuba, it was also about the workers of Britain, showing what creative sweep and ingenuity from workers in all parts of the country and all parts of the union movement could do if it really put its minds to it.

"Salud" was created—a trade union organization aiming to fill a huge ship with everything that the Cubans needed. While the skeptics scoffed and made themselves scarce at the thought of too much work, the organization quickly filled with enthusiastic trade unionists and workers, who often had a specific knowledge of some part of the equipment needed.

Numerous unions began to get involved, including general unions such as UNISON, TGWU and GMB, as well as more specialized ones such as the firefighters in the FBU and teachers in the NUT. The objective was the broadest possible support from British workers for the people of Cuba—not token political gestures and posturizing slogans but equipment that would save and change lives.

The logistical problems remained huge but help came from all quarters. The International Rescue Corps, a group of British volunteers who have assisted in relief efforts in all parts of the world, volunteered their time and experience.

Experts in logistics stepped forward, as well as others who had almost mystical powers to turn tired equipment back into useful working machinery.

On the shipping front a friendly shipping agent emerged—a Dutch-Cuban joint venture with the know-how to deal with ports, customs, bills of lading, ship's manifest and other arcane but vital matters. The request for help was cast wider and wider, with surprising results.

The initial offers were astonishing. Ambulances from the London Ambulance Service, 50 buses from all over the country, fire engines from the north east and Norfolk. On the medical front, a vast array of good, working medical equipment began to build up, stores of useful medicines as well as food, clothing, shoes, etc.

The net was widened; employers' organizations including public services, were approached. The sheer nerve and the scale of the project, derided as to its anticipated downfall, turned out to be its salvation. Everyone wanted to be part of what was shaping up as a little piece of history. The wider the support base grew, the more the organizers dared to ask of anyone who stood still long enough. Thompsons, one of Britain's foremost firms of solicitors, joined in, providing valuable support.

As the year progressed, stockpiled aid began to amass across Britain. Buses and ambulances were stashed near Barnsley by the National Union of Mineworkers. More buses were collected at Grangemouth. A printing press from London, medical equipment in Derby and Oxford, railway uniforms from Newcastle jostled for space with ten tons of milk from Carlisle. A thousand tires collected by the Yorkshire NUM and the Cuba Solidarity Campaign, which dovetailed its long-standing container appeal with the ever-growing mountain of useful items.

As the enthusiasm for the project grew, support ranged from those who admired Cuba's independent spirit to those who had simply enjoyed a holiday there and remembered the warmth of its people. A press and media campaign fronted by the actors of the TV series *Casualty* attracted even more offers.

One year after they had stared at a single beaten-up bus the organizers returned to Cuba to finalize arrangements with the Ministry of Health, the CTC, and the Health trade union SNTS. A final timetable was agreed. All sides would aim to get the ship to Cuba for 26 July, the Cubans' national day.

The Port of Liverpool agreed to help the project and tons of equipment started to arrive from all over Britain. More equipment arrived. And more. But no ship. Weeks passed and the Port of Liverpool grew increasingly anxious. Was this a real event, or was it going to implode?

Those who had sneered from the start suddenly reemerged to crow at the imminent downfall of another big idea.

In July, the Salud Executive visited Havana. In a meeting embracing about a third of Cuba's ministers of state a series of obstacles were removed.

The designated ship was docked in Poland, half loaded. The Poles had stopped loading and were unwilling or unable to explain. Some of those at the meeting favored the cock-up theory of history, while others preferred conspiracy. Some saw the hand of the CIA, displeased at such a stylish attempt to puncture their blockade and determined to rain on the Cubans' parade.

The Cubans responded by pursuing legal redress against the Polish port authorities. The meeting, chaired by General Secretary Pedro Ross, decided to do whatever it took to divert the ship to Liverpool. The Health Ministry would not let down all the people who had contributed. In the end costs were turning out to be even lower than predicted as compensation rolled in from Poland.

In August 1999 the *Luric Island*, diverted from St. Petersburg, docked in Liverpool. Solidarity proved powerful as the venture brought together the TGWU, the sacked Liverpool dockers and unionised stevedores along with the Merseyside Dock and Harbour Board. The Cuban ship began to be loaded.

Few people who witnessed the loading can doubt the possibility of progress in Britain. Watching aid workers removing and replacing a cracked ambulance windscreen with nothing more than a Swiss Army knife restores your faith in ingenuity. The Liverpool Dockers rallied round, including those who fulfilled a childhood wish to be a fireman, racing around the docks in the donated fire engines with sirens wailing. Bus enthusiasts turned up, impressed by the range and condition of the donated buses. They stayed to help the dockers drive the vehicles on board.

The ship was finally loaded with a thousand tons of aid from workers and organizations representing every aspect of life in Britain.

To celebrate, UNISON and the Merseyside Cuba Solidarity Campaign threw a party for the crew and those involved. On 26 August 1999 the *Luric Island* set sail for Cuba. The Cubans may occasionally leave things to the eleventh hour, but they always come through and sometimes the British working people do the same. Every single person who contributed to Salud in any way shared the victory of making this event happen, not only for Cuba but also for British workers rediscovering what their unity of purpose can do.

Two British Communists took the idea of solidarity aid and, on a scale never seen before within the British trade union movement, set in motion with the aid of many others what was to be the first of several ships for Cuba. Trade unions changed their policies to support Cuba. Even the British Trades Union Congress, historic and servile follower of the line of the US trade unions, changed its position to one of support. The idea of solidarity, worker-to-worker support, manifested itself as a material force as British workers and their trade unions grasped the idea. As much as the Cuban working class through its Labor Parliaments had risen to the challenge of the "Special Period in times of peace," so British workers rose to the challenge of sending material aid to Cuba and hence breaching the blockade.

Ideas with organization, commitment, and ideological clarity change the world. The Cuban Labor Parliaments were one such idea in the rich lexicon of ideas from revolutionary Cuba.

Acknowledgments and thanks for all the labor input into creating this publication:

Linda Perks, Richard Mann, Kevin Russell, Gilda Chacon (CTC National Havana), Mauricio Ross.

—CHRIS REMINGTON
RETIRED REGIONAL HEAD OF HEALTH UNISON LONDON
[*personal capacity*]

PART ONE

A BRIEF INTRODUCTION

AMONG CUBAN MEN AND WOMEN older than thirty-five, or anyone who lived in Cuba at the beginning of the 1990s, memories persist of the challenging times called the Special Period and how, facing great adversity, the Cuban people waged a heroic resistance. What perhaps is not as well known is that this always has been true of Cuban history. Ever since the nation's founding, the inhabitants of this marvelous archipelago have responded to crises with resilience and resistance.

In confronting the challenges of that time, we in Cuba benefited from the previous three decades of having fought for and having won our independence and sovereignty. Although there have been errors and setbacks, a monumental work was in progress, whose defense, preservation, and continued development entailed great sacrifice. Under these exceptional circumstances, Commander in Chief Fidel Castro Ruz presided over the closing ceremony of the Sixteenth Congress of *Central de Trabajadores de Cuba* (Cuban Workers' Central/CTC, Cuba's labor union), held January 24–28, 1990. And although Fidel said that he had not thought to publicly proclaim the Special Period, the Congress's environment was so revolutionary and combative, with attendees wearing their militia uniforms, that he decided to raise the issue:

We also see a new generation of trade union leaders, representing a working class that is much more prepared, educated, political, and revolutionary as at any time in our history: a mass of working-class delegates.

As I suggested yesterday the Congress takes place in the middle of a universal confusion, and it is important to have a clear mind and clear ideas in a moment of universal confusion. I don't know if it was correct to speak of universal confusion, since the confusion at present exists mainly in the progressive field, in the field of the truly democratic ideas; because the imperialists are not confused, the capitalists are not confused, and they know, perfectly, what they are putting at risk in these moments.

We do not doubt that we are making the greatest efforts to do things right. We have not the slightest doubt that we are rectifying many things, nor about how we have to do it: not in a precipitous manner, but by taking concrete steps in each of the fundamental aspects of life for the development of the country. Working as we are today, we could practically do whatever we set for ourselves as goals.

Regarding the problematic phase looming ahead, the Commander in Chief stated: "There might occur other eventualities for which we need to prepare. We call this period of total blockade a 'Special Period' in wartime. But now, we have to prepare ourselves and plan for a Special Period in peacetime."

What does a Special Period in peacetime mean? Given our relationships with Eastern European countries and certain factors and processes underway in the Soviet Union, the problems might become so severe that our country would face an exceedingly difficult supply situation. Bear in mind that all our fuel comes from the Union of Soviet Socialist Republics (USSR). A one-third or one-half reduction [of the supply], or a complete cutoff, would be equivalent to a wartime situation. This, of course, would not be so grave during peacetime because there still would be possibilities for exports and imports. We must foresee the worst situation the country could face in a Special Period in peacetime, and what we must do.

Surmounting a harsh Special Period with all its complexity and possible consequences requires profound and rigorous study of the historical and the social sciences. The research presented in this book preserves the history of the period. It offers a guide to the political methodology and strategy to ensure democratic participation in the bodies that Fidel called the "workers' parliaments."

The disappearance of the Soviet Union and the European socialist bloc resulted in a political and ideological crisis with seismic repercussions, devastating for the revolutionary and progressive movement worldwide and in Cuba, mainly in the economic sphere. The situation in which Cuba found itself was like a house painter who suddenly has the ladder pulled out from under him and is left hanging. This abrupt and immense loss of supplies, markets, and sources of finance, along with the worsening of the blockade implemented by the United States, represented a devastating blow. It was inevitable that Cuba would have to urgently adopt measures that demanded great sacrifices, both personal and collective. They would include the postponement of plans and programs for economic and social development. This had to be done to preserve the essential achievements of the Revolution in education, public health, and social security. There was no other way to defend the Revolution's foundations and to continue to build on them.

Yes, there would be many painfully restrictive measures. But they would not be imposed by government decree, and they certainly would never be neoliberal. They would result from broad and profound consultation with the entire country, including agricultural workers, students, and the general population. The National Assembly of People's Power adopted this approach, which led to the establishment of the workers' parliaments during the first months of 1994.

This unprecedented democratic and participatory process produced results that exceeded the most optimistic expectations. It elicited the commitment and the creativity essential to developing feasible proposals for surviving the Special Period. This book will describe how the process unfolded, with data, documentation, testimonies, and concepts discussed in our press.

This book presents essential information about our revolutionary work and its internationalist aspect during this period. The book will contrast this information with data showing the enormous economic setbacks in the Cuban economy, worsened by the intensified blockade (which remains in force). For more than a quarter of a century, from 1992 to 2017, the international community voted overwhelmingly in favor of the draft resolution that Cuba has annually presented to the General Assembly of the United Nations demanding an end "to the economic, commercial, and financial blockade imposed by the United States of America against Cuba." Of the twenty-seven times that the resolution has been up for a vote, the United States and Israel voted against it twenty-six times, except for 2015, when they abstained.

In this last year, 2017, the U.S. General Assembly delegation made clear that the administration of President Donald Trump would continue to interfere in Cuba's affairs, dismantling the breakthroughs in relations, however limited, achieved between Cuba and the United States during the presidency of Barack Obama.

The Trump administration created new obstacles to normalized relations between the United States and Cuba. These include disinformation campaigns, such as the so-called sonic attacks that purportedly caused health problems in U.S. diplomats in Havana. This false allegation became the justification for the withdrawal of 60 percent of the U.S. embassy personnel and Cuban diplomats' expulsion from Cuba's Washington embassy offices in 2017. The Trump administration took these actions despite the critical statements of influential U.S. scientists and of other governments that rejected these allegations.

The gestation and development of the workers' parliaments took place in the early 1980s. During this period, the United States devised an aggressive, anti-socialist strategy, mainly focused on eliminating the Cuban example. At the time, the Cuban Revolution was going through a phase of institutionalization while correcting errors. Meanwhile, dramatic events were occurring that put paid to the very existence of the European socialist bloc and the Soviet Union.

To grasp what was occurring during this period, an overall understanding of the Cuban historical process is essential. This is why this book was conceived in two parts. The first addresses the experience of the workers' parliaments. The second aims to synthesize the events shaping the Cuban historical fabric and demonstrate the core features of our intentions and purpose.

The intention is not to present a history of Cuba but to help readers, especially those unfamiliar with the period under discussion, to understand the Cuban reality. The book captures the thinking of Cuba's workers and the general population during the most challenging moments of the Special Period. It describes how they created an authentically democratic mechanism, the workers' parliaments. It also describes the sacrifices made under difficult circumstances, focusing on the creativity, resilience, and resistance that Cubans demonstrated.

I will leave it to my readers to judge whether the book achieves these goals.

WHY WORKERS' PARLIAMENTS?

The primary purpose of this book is to explain the development and organization of the workers' parliaments. Their origins lie in speeches by Fidel Castro and other materials and articles published in the *Trabajadores* newspaper, records of the National Assembly of People's Power, and the author's archives. There is also a bibliography at the end of the book.

The Santa Fe Program

In 1981, Ronald Reagan became the fortieth president of the United States. Reagan, an ultra-conservative, pursued a foreign policy of intransigent hostility toward the Soviet Union and the Cuban Revolution. The Santa Fe Program set forth policy directions of the new administration toward Latin America and Cuba. Reagan received the initial draft of the policy in May 1980, six months before the presidential election.

The main points of the document included the setting up of governments whose positions were close to that of the United States, with limited management capacity and dependent on advisors sent by the American government; the promotion of neoliberal economic reforms

24   HOW THE WORKERS' PARLIAMENTS

to facilitate U.S. investments in Latin American countries while undermining local economies; undercutting left-wing intellectuals and others critical of the United States while providing platforms to pro-American intellectuals and politicians; using campaigns against drug trafficking to enhance the U.S. military presence and to finance paramilitary groups; the destabilization of Latin American traditional cultures and left-wing popular movements; and financing and promoting fundamentalist, evangelical Christianity to undermine political movements and channel popular demands toward religious activism.

Reagan overturned measures modifying the blockade enacted by the Gerald Ford and Jimmy Carter administrations. Reagan then intensified the blockade, expanding it by propaganda designed to foment internal subversion and increase international pressure on Cuba. Around the same time, the Soviet Union unexpectedly told Cuba that it would not come to its aid if the United States imposed a military blockade or bombed or invaded.

Perestroika

When in 1985 the USSR's last president, Mikhael Gorbachev, initiated *perestroika* (restructuring),[1] the socialist bloc was manifesting significant weaknesses. They included the proliferation of social ills, the influence of "Western" concepts and ideas in specific sectors of the Soviet society, repudiation of a rich and legitimate history, inefficient investment, decreased labor productivity, and the end of collaboration within the framework of the Council for Mutual Economic Aid (COMECON).[2]

José Luis Rodríguez, PhD, a researcher and former minister of economics and planning, has analyzed Eastern European events that portended capitalism's return and the rise to power of anti-socialist forces. The causes include the complexity of socialist construction and errors committed in building socialism.

The collapse of the socialist bloc meant that some states swallowed other states, the working class lost power, and capitalist restoration got underway. Socialism was no longer on the agenda, replaced by a focus on market economies. The prevailing voices favored capitalism— the most classic, unregulated capitalism—and the USSR´s Communist Party was outlawed and dissolved by decree. Events were occurring at rapid speed, and the consequences of the disintegration of that great, multinational state were becoming evident.

As the problems worsened, Cuba quickly restructured its economic relations with the Soviet Union under new conditions. It had to undertake the third significant economic reform of its commercial trade since the late nineteenth century, with its main trade partners changing from Spain to the United States, and, until 1990, the Soviet Union.

The USSR, the European socialist countries, China, and the Cuban Revolution changed the global political balance. In the 1980s, however, the forces of capital, led by the governments of Ronald Reagan in the United States and Margaret Thatcher in the United Kingdom, launched a counteroffensive to impose their conditions. The breakup of the European socialist bloc was the immediate antecedent of the much worse crisis unleashed in the second half of that decade.

A Special Period

These events led Cuba's leadership to identify measures to respond to a naval or air blockade. Cuba also responded by declaring a Special Period in wartime. To that end, it was necessary to inform the Cuban people of the gravity of the situation and involve them, particularly workers, in responding to the challenges it presented.

A major priority was to provide information, direction, and orientation to the population, especially to the workers, about imminent problems. To explain their causes and to involve the people in this new phase full of challenges demanded resilience and determination in defense of the political and social project of the Revolution.

Fidel Castro's leadership played an essential role in this process. In his contact with workers' collectives and the general population, his eloquent words, sound arguments, optimism, and confidence in the face of the severe limitations that would affect Cuba, expressed the brilliance of his strategic thought.

FIDEL SAW IT COMING

On July 26, 1989, in a ceremony celebrated in the Camagüey province to commemorate the assaults on the Moncada fortress and Carlos Manuel de Céspedes (hero of Cuba's first independence movement), Fidel expressed his optimism for what had been created during the years of revolution. He analyzed the approaching threats and dangers. Using Camagüey as his reference point, he explained how much progress the Revolution had made in education and public health. Regarding the economy, he cited advances in electric power generation, the chemical and mechanical industries, construction materials, food and sugar production. He spoke about the mechanization and modernization of agriculture, road and railway construction, and ports, dams, and micro-dams. Additionally, he discussed new developments in science, culture, and sports. These advances, he noted, were the results of three decades of transformation throughout Cuba.

During that speech, he also addressed significant global issues—debt, economic crisis, and especially the impact of the historical moment on the world's socialist and revolutionary movements.

He stated that in the mid-1980s those global issues significantly affected life in Cuba. He went on to analyze the impact of those realities: "We cannot even say with certainty that the supplies from the socialist bloc that have been arriving in our country for almost thirty years with the punctuality of a watch will continue to arrive."[3]

He explained how all of this was occurring with the blessing of the United States, which saw the socialist world in decline. In the U.S. empire's view, the disintegration of socialism meant that Cuba would not survive. Hence the increased U.S. hostility toward the Cuban Revolution.

Fidel, cognizant of the difficulties and conflicts that were emerging in the Soviet Union, stated: "If tomorrow or any other day we wake up to the news of civil conflict in the USSR, or even that the USSR has disintegrated, which we hope never happens, even in those circumstances, Cuba and the Cuban Revolution would keep on fighting and would keep on resisting!"[4]

SAVED THE CUBAN REVOLUTION 27

Various observers have noted that Cuba's foreign trade during this period was in a state similar to that of 1962 when the United States declared the economic blockade. But in the new period, Cuba was being subjected to a double blockade: the one the United States had imposed in 1962 and continued to reinforce, and one generated by the collapse of the Cuban markets in Eastern Europe and the USSR.

A CONGRESS IN MILITARY UNIFORMS

In his closing speech to the Sixteenth Congress of the CTC, Fidel pointed out that the event was occurring during "the most decisive stage in the history of the Revolution." It also was taking place during a time of widespread confusion "in the progressive field, in genuinely democratic thought, in socialist and revolutionary thinking."

The CTC leadership called on the 2,515 democratically elected delegates (from among more than 64,000 pre-candidates proposed in the basic assemblies) to attend the Congress sessions in the uniform of the Milicias de Tropas Territoriales (Territorial Troop Militias/MTT; the MTT were created in response to the threats of imperial aggression). "I think it was an excellent idea that you came with your militia uniforms," he said.

Fidel stressed the importance of workers and their representatives in fighting to defend "the interests of the whole society, regardless of the peculiarities and problems of any particular sector." Popular unity, he emphasized, was what the country was defending from the U.S. empire. "We will never allow anything," he said, "that weakens the unity of the people, that divides our people."

WHAT IS A SPECIAL PERIOD IN PEACETIME?

At the Congress, Fidel introduced the concept of the Special Period in peacetime:

> What does a Special Period in peacetime mean? That economic problems have become so severe because of relations with Eastern

European countries, or could become, because of developments in the Soviet Union, so severe that our country would face a challenging supply situation. Bear in mind that the fuel supplied by the Soviet Union might be reduced by a third or halved because of difficulties there, or even reduced to zero, which would be equivalent to what we would call a Special Period in wartime.

Our people have been preparing for years against certain dangers. For ten years, we have been strengthening our defenses. We have been applying the people's concept of war. We have drawn up plans for all eventualities, beginning with the country's total military blockade, in which case not a single bullet could reach here. We knew this before the current issues of the U.S. empire's superiority in conventional weapons, the air and naval superiority, which would make it impossible for a single bullet to arrive from outside. Now we have to prepare for all these problems and even plan for a Special Period in peacetime.

It was a matter of not only confronting challenges to survival but also of maintaining the country's development. There would be no turning back in such vital areas as hydraulic capacity, the pharmaceutical industry, biotechnology, and foreign currency resources such as tourism. Castro set forth some inviolable principles: the defense of national sovereignty; the preservation of the achievements of the Revolution in health, education, and social equality; and the right to employment, along with the maintenance of a revolutionary ethic, the moral and spiritual values forged in the years of building a new society.

THE FOURTH PARTY CONGRESS AND THE START OF THE SPECIAL PERIOD

In the inaugural session of the Fourth Party Congress on October 10, 1991, Fidel Castro discussed Cuba's problems and what was needed to overcome them. He referred to programs begun during the process of "rectification" that had to be interrupted.[5] He spoke about achievements in the construction of new housing and the microbrigade movement in which small groups of worker volunteers constructed urban housing; the production of construction materials; the considerable and accelerated investments in cement production capacity for housing, for economic works, and for hotels; expanded production capacity for steel bars, blocks, bricks, sand, and tiles. He also spoke about organizing dozens of brigades to build dams and canals, and contingents of builders; drawing up agricultural production plans, building cowsheds, pig farms, poultry houses, and rice engineering systems.

The disappearance of the socialist field from Eastern Europe and the USSR's disintegration had a devastating impact on the Cuban economy. Gross domestic product fell by nearly 35 percent. Cuba lost more than 70 percent of its foreign markets. The oil supply fell from 13 million tons to 5.8 million. In 1990, 3 billion rubles in products were no longer received.

Critics of the Cuban Revolution spoke of "the end of history," that capitalism had proved to be the best of all possible systems. Some predicted that the Revolution would expire in a matter of weeks. In 1990, the effects of what was happening in the Soviet Union were already being felt. That year, goods valued at 1.3 billion rubles, including 3.3 million tons of fuel, were no longer being received as planned.

At the Fourth Party Congress, Fidel explained that Cuba's agreements with the USSR no longer had five-year terms but were reduced to twelve months. They also would be measured in dollars and not in rubles. Sugar prices had fallen, which reduced Cuba's purchasing power by one billion dollars. The USSR set its 1991 exports at $3.94 billion, almost $1.20 billion less than the previous year. Oil deliveries from the Soviet Union fell to a maximum of 10 million tons, from the 13 million previously received.

Cuba had to concentrate on what was important—ensuring essential programs and producing such items as televisions, radios, refrigerators, fans, automobiles, and agricultural equipment, while reducing others to a minimum, such as transport equipment.

MEASURES TO ADDRESS THE CRISIS

Under these conditions, the country's leadership had to adopt measures to readjust the economy, to ensure the minimum requirements for its existence and vitality.

In 1992, the Constitution was modified to consider new forms of ownership, including the emergence of self-employment, the creation of agricultural markets, and the conversion from state-owned to agrarian cooperatives. The state monopoly on foreign trade was eliminated; Cuba opened up to foreign capital; state-owned and foreign companies were permitted to engage in trade. Cuba enacted a Business Improvement and Foreign Investment Law; launched new programs in nontraditional sectors such as tourism, biotechnology, communications, information technology, and specialized services, such as environmental impact studies and scientific research. There also was revitalization of traditional sectors: tobacco, coffee, seafood, alcoholic beverages, sugar, and nickel, all of which continue to be important exports.

The possession of dollars was decriminalized, and a retail market in foreign currency emerged. Scientific research took off as a generator of consumer goods. From that moment on, the entire economy deteriorated, with disastrous effects on all sectors of society, with 1993 and 1994 becoming the most critical and difficult years of this stage. Hundreds of factories were closed, thousands of workers were sent home, albeit with a 70 percent wage guarantee; in the capital alone, the 32,000 daily trips made by urban buses fell to less than 10,000; electricity was provided for only twelve hours a day, and on the warm summer nights people could be seen sleeping on rooftops and doorways or sitting outside the houses looking for ventilation.

ENEMY ENCOURAGEMENT OF SOCIAL INDISCIPLINE AND VANDALISM

In these circumstances, social indiscipline and acts of vandalism increased, such as throwing stones and bottles in the streets, sabotage of public transportation and institutions, destruction of state property,

SAVED THE CUBAN REVOLUTION   31

hijacking of boats and airplanes, illegal departures from the country, all encouraged by the government of the United States and the anti-Cuban "mafia"—for example, terrorist Cuban defectors and their enablers living in Miami in the service of the empire. At the same time, plagues were introduced from abroad to destroy agricultural production and livestock. The epidemic of hemorrhagic dengue fever cost the lives of more than a hundred children. These attacks were intended to provoke chaos, discouragement, a sense of an out-of-control crisis.

These events were not simply the results of the deteriorating economy and the drastic reduction of the population's standard of living because of the European socialist collapse. The manifestations of violence and criminality were a direct consequence of U.S. policy to destroy the Revolution. They were also fostered by the United States reducing legal options to emigrate. The Cuban Adjustment Act, passed by the U.S. Congress in 1959, privileged Cuban immigration for political purposes. This was enhanced by the restriction on the granting of visas and the encouragement of illegal immigration, stimulated and favored by the "wet and dry feet" law that admitted those who managed to reach any portion of U.S. territory regardless of the means they had used to do so. In 1996, the U.S. government introduced the so-called "wet feet, dry feet policy," which reduced the application of the act.

Likewise, anti-Cuba legislation such as the Torricelli Law[6] was enacted in 1992 to reinforce the blockade and creating Trojan horses to undermine popular resistance and bring about the collapse of the Cuban political system from within. These policies reached delirious extremes, such as the Helms-Burton Act of 1996.[7]

FIDEL MEETS THE PEOPLE

On August 5, 1994, riots and other disorders broke out in Havana, initially near the port and in Central Havana and Old Havana. Cubans responded by marching to the scenes and confronting the rioters. Police units mobilized to establish order. Fidel made an appearance, giving instructions that no weapons should be used against the rioters. He took on the political confrontation, relying on his moral authority

32 HOW THE WORKERS' PARLIAMENTS

and the force of reason and argument, in the face of confusion and even enemy attempts to pay demonstrators to generate acts of violence.

As soon as the protesters noticed Castro's presence, they began to disperse and retreat.

That evening, when asked by journalists about his presence where the events were taking place, Fidel replied, "If some stones were really being thrown and there was some shooting, I wanted to get my share of stones and shooting, too." He also argued that he had a special interest "in talking with our people, to exhort them to be calm, patient, cold-blooded, and not to let themselves be provoked."

Fidel spoke about how the United States believed that the Cuban Revolution would collapse soon after the collapse of the socialist camp. He explained that the U.S. strategy employed many mechanisms to undermine the Cuban economy, to foment popular discontent, and to stimulate an exodus by illegal means, while at the same time minimizing or nullifying the possibilities of legal, safe, and orderly emigration.

THE PEOPLE RESPOND

The Special Period also affected Cubans' health through a significant decrease in protein consumption and an acute lack of medication. But even in these extreme conditions, with overwhelming shortages of food, transportation, electricity, and practically every other essential, Cuban women re-created the biblical miracle of multiplying bread and fish to sustain their families. No schools were closed, nor did the health centers stop providing services. Teachers, doctors, nurses, and other workers from various sectors continued to perform with few resources.

Especially significant was the introduction and promotion of the bicycle as an important means of transporting people, especially in the cities. In record time, the country acquired one million bicycles from China, which students at technological education centers assembled. Workers from large factories made an essential contribution to addressing the transportation crisis affecting all of Cuban society.

Tens of thousands of workers, men and women, from enterprises that had shut down machinery or reduced their activity because of

SAVED THE CUBAN REVOLUTION   33

shortages of fuel, raw materials, and other inputs, made their way to the
fields. They brought such rustic tools as the primitive *coa*—a pointed
hardwood stick for drilling into the soil—the hoe, animal traction, and
the *mambí* machete, now a new productive tool, to reaffirm their will
to resist and win. Workers were trained as oxen handlers all over the
country. Equipment such as yokes and harnesses were manufactured.
Numerous work centers, institutions, and organizations requested
plots of land for agricultural production for their workers' cafeterias,
to feed their families, and for children's circles, schools, and health
facilities.

"IT IS EASIER TO FIND A DINOSAUR CROSSING THE STREET THAN A PUMPKIN IN THE MARKET"

Workers at the Ranchuelos cigar factory in Villa Clara observed that
"it was easier to find a dinosaur crossing this street than a pumpkin
in the market." When these workers were asked why they had not created, as had been done elsewhere, a garden to supply food to workers
and their families, they replied that they had attempted to do so, in the
municipality and the province, but their efforts were unsuccessful. The
Minister of Agriculture, Alfredo Jordán Morales, helped to resolve that
issue. The cigar workers were assigned a plot of unused land that was
relatively close to the factory, and they quickly put it into production.
The Cubans called their solution "organoponics" because it uses an
organic substrate, obtained from crop residues, household wastes, and
animal manure.[8] With the Special Period's onset, organoponic gardens
proved ideal for growing crops on poor soil in small urban spaces. A
typical organoponic garden is started by making furrows in the soil,
then lining the rows with protective barriers of wood, stone, bricks,
or concrete. The soil quality is gradually improved by incorporating
organic matter. As organic content increases, so do the levels of soil
nutrients and moisture (and the height of the bed). Organoponics—
the term applies to the technology and the gardens themselves—can
be implemented at building sites, vacant lots, and roadsides, and in
terraces on sloping land. Soil can be adapted to grow particular crops.

If the soil is affected by nematodes or fungi, the entire substrate can be replaced.

Among the first organoponic gardens were those created on military airstrips, one in the mountains of the historic Frank País II Eastern Front, commanded by Raúl Castro during the struggle against Batista, and the other in the current Ciudad Libertad, formerly Camp Columbia, the main military fortress, which had been converted into a large school. It previously housed the General Staff of the Revolutionary Air Force. On the eve of the Bay of Pigs attack, the U.S.-backed mercenary forces dropped bombs on its runway. But thirty-one years later, vegetables were being grown on the same runway. This technique was extended to areas around military units and later to work centers throughout the country.

Soil-cement and other traditional techniques were introduced to build homes with less cement and fuel consumption. Natural and traditional medicines were promoted and extended in their use, which has also been systematically disseminated by radio up to now.

IT WAS NOT THE FIRST TIME

The Cuban people had to endure shortages and other difficulties before the Special Period. In the early 1960s, when the U.S. empire escalated its attempts to subvert the Revolution, the blockade began to have negative repercussions in the country: banditry, pirate attacks, ship hijacking, aggression emanating from the U.S. naval base in Guantánamo, attempts to assassinate Cuban leaders, and various types of sabotage ensued.

In the beginning and in the most challenging moments of the Special Period, the Rebel Army's combative legacy was evident, embodied in the exemplary and effective performance of the Revolutionary Armed Forces (FAR). The FAR excelled in their primary task of safeguarding the country's defense and providing creative and practical solutions to the economic problems. "Since the triumph of the Revolution, there has not been an economic shock or a natural disaster in which the armed forces were not at the side of our people, side by side."

SAVED THE CUBAN REVOLUTION

The then-Minister of the Armed Forces, General of the Army Raúl Castro Ruz, made four demands of the military cadres: high political, ideological, and moral qualities; highly professional preparation; mastery of the rudiments of agricultural food production; and mastery of the fundamental aspects of the economy—that is, to know where every peso spent comes from and whether the investment is justified.[9]

In an August 3, 1994, speech, Raúl Castro Ruz, in his capacity as Minister of the Armed Forces, said, "Today, as the Commander in Chief has just said . . . the main strategic, economic, political, ideological, and military task that all Cuban revolutionaries have without exception . . . is to guarantee food for the population. Yesterday we said that beans were worth as much as guns; today we say that beans are worth more than guns."[10]

Of great importance in those years was the extension of agricultural practices being applied by the Ministry of the Revolutionary Armed Forces, under the leadership of Raúl Castro, who later became president of the State and Ministerial Councils, such as the Business Improvement Council.[11] The development of urban agriculture included the creation of gardens in workplaces, hospitals, schools, neighborhoods, and the cultivation of medicinal plants and their use in medical practice, among others.

"YES, WE CAN"

In the late 1980s and early 1990s, work proceeded on major projects despite the Special Period's challenges. Facilities for the Pan-American Games of 1991 included lodging for the athletes and the Expo Cuba Fairgrounds, and factories for the construction industry were also built. There were impressive achievements in the health sector, with an increase in hospital beds and the expansion of several existing hospitals. The creation of the Scientific Pole, with the Center for Genetic Engineering and Biotechnology; the Carlos J. Finlay Institute; the Institute of Immunoassay; and the Institute of Monoclonal Antibodies were also notable additions.

Fidel Castro encouraged all these efforts. He would show up at sites at any hour of the day or night, his presence inspiring the workers. This was his personal style to link directly with the labor groups, to have an ongoing dialogue with the people, and to learn about their work and their concerns.

These were years of arduous work by the Cuban people and the leadership of the Revolution, with in-depth and systematic analysis of each step, which imbued in everyone confidence that the country's demanding situations would be overcome. Under the direction of Raúl Castro, meetings were held with leading cadres in the eastern, central, and western territories. The attendees analyzed the subjective issues—such as confusion and defeatism—that were exacerbating the material challenges facing the country.

WHY DO UNIONS EXIST?

It was essential that the Cuban people and workers understood the country's circumstances and not lose confidence in the revolutionary process and its aims of justice and equity. Above all, Cubans had to recognize that the exceptional situation demanded everyone's efforts to save the socialist project and further develop it.

We in the labor movement felt that it was time to rethink specific questions. Why do unions exist? What should distinguish us in functions, language, methods, and style from the administrative apparatus? This was the moment to strengthen the union bases so that they would represent the specific interests of the workers and be organizationally and politically prepared to play a decisive role in moments of crisis.

In this regard, we in the *Central de Trabajadores de Cuba* (Cuban Workers' Central/CTC) reiterated that the workers in our society are the owners and their own employees. So the union structures could not in any way turn a blind eye to the negative attitudes of workers and managers who did not fulfill their duties. Nor could they remain silent in the face of errors, inadequacies, and unfounded claims by those who did not adopt positions that were consistent with the situation facing the country. It was a matter of preparing to confront without ideological regression the realities that at times conflicted with principles we should not abandon and that we had always considered sacred.

It was necessary to refine our intelligence and sensitivity to project ourselves effectively in the face of the realities that have come about and their evolution. We remembered Jose Martí's assertion that "one fights when one prepares armies for battle."

At this crucial hour of the Cuban Revolution, we in the CTC were making it clear to the workers that there was no point in waiting to wage a struggle that had its strategy well laid out.

Fidel's work explaining, giving arguments, promoting ideas and actions, with that exemplary quality that characterized his style of communication, and to convince, to teach, was tireless. In all his speeches of that period, he insisted on the need to recognize that what was happening in Cuba transcended its borders, stating that the Revolution had not developed independently from the rest of the world and its problems.

ANALYSIS, MEASURES, ACTIONS

At the same time, the measures Fidel discussed on July 26, 1993, were being applied. These included the decriminalization of the use of foreign currency and the creation of a commercial network to recover it for social policies; the promotion of tourism as an immediate source of income; the reorganization of agriculture through the creation of the Basic Units of Cooperative Production (BUCP); the authorization of self-employment under certain rules; and the promotion of foreign investment.

The Cuban government continued to seek viable solutions to the serious problem of excess money circulating in the country, derived in part from the revolutionary policy of maintaining salaries and pensions even without an adequate supply of consumer goods to absorb these funds. As Fidel explained at the 1993 Moncada commemoration in Santiago de Cuba:

> Among other factors, it is imperative to face the question of excess

circulating money. . . . We had the most excess circulation in 1970; there were around 3.5 billion pesos in circulation. Of course, the economy also grew after those years. Still, today's working capital is three times greater than in 1970, at around 9 billion pesos. In 1970, it was possible to find ways to reduce that excess of money in circulation, ways that are not available to us today. Why did the circulation grow so considerably? Simply because even in a Special Period, the Revolution was not willing, is not willing, and will not be willing, to sacrifice the people.

THE SECOND ORDINARY SESSION OF THE NATIONAL ASSEMBLY OF PEOPLE'S POWER

The thorny issue of excess circulation was on the agenda of the Second Ordinary Session of the National Assembly of People's Power in its Fourth Legislature, held December 26–28, 1993. There were extensive discussions with the deputies in each province to ensure that they were well informed and prepared for the debates in the assembly.

Minister José Luis Rodríguez made it clear that the financial imbalance was one of the most severe economic, political, and social problems that the country was facing. In 1989, this excess reached 4.163 billion pesos. In 1993, it exceeded 10 billion, equivalent to fourteen months of average monthly salary. By the end of that year, it was projected that the excess would continue to increase, generating more inflation. And without a doubt, this was a factor that discouraged work. However, it also represented an inequality because the distribution of this money was not fair. Some had too much; others lived from day to day.

Despite this, we could not fail to recognize the exemplary attitude of the majority of our compatriots. Faced with this discouragement and significant material shortages, they worked hard, demonstrating their revolutionary spirit and their capacity for heroic resistance to protect the Revolution.

Between 1989 and 1992, goods and services had fallen by 35 percent, which, together with the supply shortages, made the excess circulating funds one of the main factors that favored the expansion of the so-called black market, where all kinds of speculative operations were carried out at exorbitant prices. The situation was aggravated by high budget deficits, which, from about 1.4 billion pesos in 1989, had risen to more than 4.2 billion pesos.

Concerning the notable drop in the country's economic activity, Fidel, in his July 26 speech in Santiago de Cuba, pointed out: "In other countries, they would have adopted the famous shock measures. In effect, these measures, typical of neoliberalism, seek a balance at any cost between supply and demand through the action of market forces—whose consequences are truly terrible for those who receive less income—by liberating prices, freezing salaries, and reducing social expenses covered by the state, among other decisions."

In Cuba, of course, this had not been the case. From 1989 to 1993, the state sector maintained the same employment. The average salary was practically unchanged. The public health budget rose by 10.3 percent, and the social security budget grew by 33.4 percent. However, subsidies to cover losses increased beyond expectations and reached 4.6 billion pesos in 1993, 73 percent more than in 1989. The imbalances were a serious obstacle to increasing economic efficiency, so it was imperative to confront them, taking into account economic, political, and social factors. This required Cuban revolutionaries to avoid technocratic approaches, to resist irresponsible and precipitous actions, and to refute superficial judgments of Cuba's complex economic situation.

It would have been desirable to increase the supply of goods and services, but this would not be possible in the short term, given the magnitude of effort required. Such a solution was applied in the early 1970s, when imports increased, which was made possible by conditions the country enjoyed at the time but which no longer existed.

It was then proposed to address the Cuban economy's financial imbalances with different methods that, without abandoning the essential principles of justice and social equity, would facilitate an adequate solution. Such solutions would require the adoption of measures that would not be applied in other conditions. Cuba's problems could not be solved with a single measure because their complex nature forced

40   HOW THE WORKERS' PARLIAMENTS

the adoption of a coherent array of actions. Solutions would not have an immediate effect and would require time. Order and discipline on everyone's part were needed more than ever to move forward.

For the Cuban state to meet the needs of its people, it would necessitate the gradual, orderly, and rational application of a new taxation system. At the same time expenditures, and especially subsidies for losses, had to be restricted as much as possible. Greater efficiency in the use of scarce resources, lower costs, increased labor productivity, and growth in production were all essential to overcoming the Special Period.

WHAT THE WORKERS SAY IN THE PARLIAMENTS

Several Congress members insisted, with different nuances, on the need to change the currency, and even to freeze high bank accounts as part of the battle against illicit enrichment and the "pots."[12] Others emphasized eliminating undue subsidies or ensuring less support from the state and increasing individuals' responsibility. It was argued that the adopted measures should be accompanied by a mass political process to gain maximum popular support. Such an initiative was needed to counter the most negative effects of the Special Period: lack of interest in work, which was expressed in high and growing absenteeism, labor indiscipline, and low productivity, as well as the exodus of workers from some critical sectors. Greater and more efficient economic activity was required, even with limited energy and fuel. It was essential to assess the basic needs of the population while also identifying waste, for example of water and electricity, whose rates were oversubsidized by the state as well as the inadequacy of other services that were either too expensive or too cheap.

Some items were priced low, like bicycles, at 150 pesos, which were being sold on the black market at 2,000 pesos and more. The need for a cigarette quota in the basic supply basket and new taxes on beer and rum were considered.

Other pressing concerns included accounts payable and receivable as a source of fund diversions and reductions, and excessive subsidies.

The new Basic Units of Agricultural Production had given rise to expectations of more food and higher incomes, as well as concerns about stockpiling and markets. The criteria for remuneration and financing of the arts sector were also discussed.

Many other ideas and proposals were presented, with supporting arguments. On many occasions, Fidel asked for details and exchanged opinions with the deputies to deepen the analysis of such topics as currency exchange, its advantages and disadvantages; the high, unjustified subsidies associated with poor management; the question of taxation; and whether cigarettes and alcoholic beverages should be removed from the *Libreta de Abastecimiento*[13] and their prices increased to collect more revenue and reduce circulating currency.

FIDEL REFLECTS, ARGUES, GIVES HIS OPINION, PROMOTES DISCUSSION

After some sixty deputies had spoken, Fidel said:

> I raised the question of whether we confiscated money, because in 1961 we confiscated the money of the bourgeoisie. They kept it outside the country; they had it in lots of places, they didn't have it in the banks. All the money in banks was respected; then some, but not all, of the money was confiscated.
>
> I talked about this, and I talked about changing it, because it is in the arsenal of possible measures. We wanted to specify taxes, quantify how much those taxes were, and how much we would collect. . . . We wanted to be specific, but since this is one of the thorniest issues in the arsenal of possible measures, that's why we wanted to talk about this, to go to the specific issues, as we have been doing in the last few hours.

Concerning a possible change of currency, he said:

> Currency change, or devaluation, are problems that are not discussed in any parliament in the world. I believe that this is the only

parliament in the world where these things are discussed as we discuss them, before you, before all the people, and before the press. We have enough courage to do that, we can do that; but that does not mean we have to stop changing currency, because if we wanted to tomorrow, we could change it. There are possible techniques for that, tomorrow, and at the cost of a few dollars. It would make no sense to raise it among the arsenal of measures if it were impracticable or something that cost so much that it was not worthwhile. As this has been said several times, I will clarify it.

He continued:

I think what we are discussing is the problem from the political point of view. Whether it is really convenient or not, whether it is possible to save it or not, what advantages it has, what disadvantages it has, and orient ourselves well, but not because it is an impossible thing.It is also in our hands to confiscate one part and not confiscate another. There are many solutions, which simply require conscience, knowledge.

One of the reasons for this discussion is that many people want the problem to be solved, to be faced. But they want to adopt hardly any of the measures that might lead to the problem's solution. And as I said, people's understanding of the measures to be taken is fundamental. . . .

It must be taken into account that we are looking for solutions for the excess of circulating currency in conditions that are not normal. Other countries, like Mexico, have devalued currency in normal conditions. They had tremendous exports, a lot of oil, and no blockade. Actually, devaluations are equivalent to confiscations of money. . . . If you have the dollar at 12.50 Mexican pesos, overnight it becomes 250; each peso has remained at 10 percent.

Devaluation is the confiscation of currency. But I will say something else: inflation is the systematic confiscation of currency. The struggle of everyday workers is such that if inflation was at least 10 percent, and they get raises of 9 or 8 percent, they lose buying power,

SAVED THE CUBAN REVOLUTION 43

and if inflation returns, they will give it again a part of that inflation, and thus they will face lower wages until they are reduced by half.

The Commander in Chief continued to elaborate on inflation:

> It is the people who have financed the infrastructure of this country, the roads, schools, and all else, and they have financed it through the *Libreta de Abastecimiento* [booklet on supplies].
>
> When there was no money to build a hospital, the hospital was always built. Ah, because there was the supplies booklet. . . . Thousands of schools were built, hundreds of hospitals, lots of things, and never a penny was added to a liter of milk, or meat, or food. I'm talking about that golden age, when what was in the supplies booklet was much more than today. I never heard anyone in this country ask if there was a budget for anything. . . . Under normal conditions, the people financed, but without inflation, as prices are not free to change; with free prices we would not have been able to do that, because with free prices we would have had price increases every month. Only once, in the Eighties, were prices of some products increased.

PEOPLE WORK BECAUSE THEY MUST

Fidel linked the excess money in circulation to the need to work:

> We have a problem, which also happened in 1970: the excess accumulation of money. . . . Here we must talk about stimulating work, and we should also talk about the need to work.
>
> I believe that collecting excess circulating currency contributes to the need for work. Stimuli are something else; there are not many we can offer, but we offer them whenever we can.
>
> We are talking about seeking financial balance and solving the problem of excess circulation when the socialist camp has disappeared. Our imports have been reduced by 78 percent, when we have the most rigorous blockade ever, during a Special Period and

44 HOW THE WORKERS' PARLIAMENTS

amid an international economic crisis. These are not the conditions in which others have faced these problems. They are much more difficult. It is a more challenging objective, but we are not afraid to debate it because the Revolution's style is precisely to do things with the people's support and understanding.

"WE HAVEN'T ALWAYS DONE THINGS RIGHT BY CONSULTING"

The Commander in Chief referred to previous experiences that were not always happy:

I remember that there was a lot of discussion about cigars and cigarettes. Because we ourselves did not agree, we decided to ask the opinion of as many people as we could, including the People's Councils: What do you think of this, what do you think of that? We haven't always done things right by consulting. I could cite examples when solutions that came from consultation were worse than other possibilities, the cigarette solution being one of them. When the problem arose that a formula had to be found to raise cigarette prices, there already was a historical quota that was languishing. We had reached certain conclusions in the Executive Committee, but when we discussed this problem in the organizing committee of the last Congress, there was no agreement or consensus on the issue.

We then decided to consult many more people, including the People's Councils. There was no agreement, no consensus. A quota on cigars was reestablished [cigars were included in the basic subsidized basket of necessary goods, the *Libreta de Abastecimiento*]. When those who had a quota were more than thirty-five years old, the crazy thing of a quota of cigars to those who were eighteen was reestablished. But since we don't have an inventory, and cannot have one, of who smokes and who doesn't smoke, it was necessary to impose a quota on all eighteen years old and up. But since many didn't smoke, they sold the cigars.

SAVED THE CUBAN REVOLUTION   45

THE SOURCES OF THE BLACK MARKET

Regarding the black market, Fidel reflected:

There are many sources of the black market. Today we have more of them: a package that comes from the United States is one, because they send new clothes or clothes for use, and the customer can sell it here at a great price. Today, the person who travels and brings back 10 kilograms of medicine—something done to help people in need, since the state does not have the resources to guarantee availability of all medicines—is seen as a formula for help, but it becomes a source of the black market.

Today, all the money remittances, and any dollar that ends up in a store, become part of the black market because any individual who receives $100 here, who buys it in the currency stores, can sell it for thousands of pesos. In other words, there are many factors today that promote the black market, not only excess money. However, excess money does quite a bit to aggravate the problem.

In short, many factors promote this situation, and we cannot have illusions; it is an evil, it is a disease with which we have to live and coexist, but we are looking for solutions in the most challenging conditions. And I believe that what we are doing is the right thing, the most honest, the most honorable thing that can be done with the people.

Fidel specified who should be well informed and who needs to be understood about these situations:

Who do we want to know about excess circulation? The people. Whose understanding do we need? From the people: those who walk around with illicit money have nothing to do; they are inventing things to do with their money. If they get nervous, they are to blame; he who does not have a clear conscience is his own problem, but I say that the honest people of this country should not have worries of any kind, even if we have to make sacrifices.

Logically, suppose any of the measures proposed here are adopted. In that case, it will mean sacrifices. . . . I don't know how some people have said that we will have to subsidize people without making commitments to subsidize. This doesn't mean that because a person who earns the minimum wage has to buy a uniform he has to go to the social security office to get a ticket and pay for the uniform. Otherwise we will never get out of that excess circulation.

Any road tax raises prices. Ah, it should be directed mainly, I think, at non-essential products. Still, any decrease in subsidies can raise the prices of some essential products. You have to see how high those prices will go and that people stop buying them. In other words, any one of these measures, even if it is small, will still mean a sacrifice for the people.

Fidel explained that it was imperative to solve the problems according to the fundamental sense of justice of the Revolution, to protect the people, to maintain the Revolution's victories, to leave no one defenseless, to not leave a recently graduated university student without a job, an average technician without a job. He stressed how much had been done to foster sugarcane recovery, of land yields, that solutions required time and sacrifices; that measures would have to be successive and inspired by certain principles. He referred to measures that were already in practice and others that were being analyzed. He observed that it was very important "to help people become more educated in an economic sense and that people help more to value everything."

At the Second Ordinary Session of the National Assembly of People's Power, Fidel emphasized the need to reach an understanding of the inevitable sacrifices so that the people would consciously support the policies to be implemented.

OUR PROPOSAL

When it seemed that the president of the assembly was about to conclude the session, we asked for the floor. A deputy and union leader, Francisco Durán Harvey, explained:

SAVED THE CUBAN REVOLUTION 47

At the end of this debate, Deputy Pedro Ross Leal, General Secretary of the Trade Union Center, suggested that the situation justified the need to develop the political process with the workers, which would first of all make possible a broad exchange "looking inward," and which in turn would promote understanding and support for the content and scope of the . . . measures to be adopted.

We proposed to carry out this overall process of explanation, clarification, and prior consultation with the workers to seek their endorsement and support of the measures that would be applied. Fidel asked how long it would take to conduct this effort. We explained that it could be done in forty-five days to two months.

"Then we would have that time to carry out the consultation while applying some measures that are already underway," Fidel said. "This legislature of the Assembly does not end here. It is now moving to the workplaces, so that the deputies and delegates to the provincial and municipal assemblies of People's Power participate with the union leaders in . . . seeking the support of the workers."

WORKERS' ASSEMBLIES INTO WORKERS' PARLIAMENTS

Fidel gave a name to the movement to convert the workers' assemblies: they would be called *workers' parliaments*. They would be a venue for workers to debate what to do at the national and local levels and to discuss problems freely and candidly. The workers' parliaments would offer them a platform to discuss their concerns, needs, and problems, and to suggest solutions. It was the formula for the direct participation of the working masses in the political elaboration of the Revolution in the critical circumstances of the Special Period. Right after the National Assembly session ended, operational discussions were held to organize and implement the process agreed upon throughout the country, after the essential coordination with the national and territorial authorities.

On January 3, 1994, we published an article in *Trabajadores* aimed at orienting and preparing the trade union movement throughout the country with the arguments necessary to undertake the broad and intense grassroots process:

> The excess money in circulation, caused largely by the permanent and growing budget deficit, is today the main concern of the Cuban family.
>
> The contraction of the national economy, suddenly provoked by external factors, has been reflected in the deterioration of individual consumption levels and in the devaluation of the purchasing power of salaries, which in many cases channel a part of income toward the black market and lessen in value every day because of the increase in those prices. As our import capacity collapsed, production went into a tailspin.... Simultaneously, the population's monetary income and the state's general expenses remained more or less stable, thus weakening the organizing feature of financial equilibrium and the motivating role of wages. However, this apparent inconsistency has guaranteed during these years of the Special Period appreciable levels of equity and social justice. It has protected each and every citizen from distress.
>
> Now the time has come to bring order to finances and to direct the efforts of society toward the harmony of state expenditure and income while actions that will reduce excess liquidity in the hands of the population are carried out.
>
> As always in our society, the workers contribute most to solving these pressing problems because no set of measures could ever hope to succeed if not supported by the knowledge, understanding, and will of the workers.
>
> Therefore, we recognize the wisdom that prevailed at the recent meeting of the National Assembly of People's Power which, while issuing a clear warning about the seriousness of economic phenomena, opted to go deeper into the essence of the main problems, to clarify the principles that are unchangeable in the face of any technical solution, and not to take new measures until the people, in particular the workers, had debated, analyzed, and understood the issues we must address in coming times.

We are convinced that the measures must be determined without haste, not only because of their technical complexity . . . but also because they must be the result of a true national consensus that does not lose sight of the sense of social justice that is the foundation of the Cuban nation.

Although we are grateful for this serene and democratic dynamic . . . we are calling for action by all workers and the trade union movement. There already is much that can be done about financial imbalance and against its causes and consequences. As Fidel has reiterated, the Cuban workers show the value of patriotic and revolutionary conscience when, every day, they defy all kinds of difficulties to fulfill their work responsibilities.

We speak of absenteeism, and there is that; we mention the exodus from one activity to others, and it occurs; we comment that some people get sick too often, and it is true. But it is undeniable that the will and commitment of the vast majority of Cuban workers are stronger than the material factors that might affect their motivation to work under the current circumstances.

Stay and improve in each center and do more with the available resources. You will be making a considerable contribution to the solution of the economic problems through greater production.

Unionism raises the ability to demand that every administration eliminate superfluous expenses and truly controls every resource so that merchandise is collected and paid for without delay, delinquency, or negligence. . . .

Fight the absurd habit of consuming without justification certain allocations, in order to ensure equal supply in the next budget cycle.

Reject inefficient management, especially where there is a possibility of safe production, because you should want to subsidize the groups that can be profitable, instead of bleeding the budget.

In 1994, sugarcane agriculture, sugar mills, and agricultural production should be at the forefront of reducing subsidies. The trade union movement supports this process with all its strength, which will be decisive for the whole country.

Today, we must strive to find practical and useful ways of action while the country develops its criteria for financial regulation. We must also encourage workers to discuss and learn about these issues, which unfortunately have been absent from popular discourse. They are not, and cannot be, the exclusive preserve of specialists.

The right of ownership would be used promptly, wherever workers and the union demand information from management about financial problems affecting the workplace.

In this way, we can identify useful measures to decrease expenses and increase income and form the collective criteria to face these problems in the present and in the future.

In a society of workers, the state must conceive and execute the budget with the same philosophy that a family does. At the time of adjustments, the family nucleus discusses and makes no sacrifice that is not good for all and ensures the welfare of all. And just as the family should not and cannot spend more than it earns, our state is also impelled to march along the strict and logical economic path.

THE CALL

In its January 10, 1994, edition, *Trabajadores* published the trade union center's call to discuss in all workers' parliaments the economic and financial issues debated in the last session of the National Assembly of People's Power. The process would occur in two stages. The first would extend for the next eighteen days, until January 28. All union leaders would participate, from the sections and bureaus at the base to the municipal unions. The second stage would include all the workers' groups in the country. Deputies and delegates to the municipal and provincial assemblies of People's Power, and leaders and other administrative officials at all levels, would participate. These assemblies in the labor centers would be the workers' parliaments.

THE PREPARATION

The first stage's preparatory meetings were attended by more than 400,000 union leaders, five for each of the 80,000 grassroots union

SAVED THE CUBAN REVOLUTION 51

sections, plus leaders from the remaining structures, including the professional cadres. These meetings provided essential insights. They also set the tone for the discussion initiated at the grassroots level. The organizing secretary of the CTC, Francisco Durán Harvey, recalls:

> Once this historic decision was approved, a program to prepare the union cadre and leaders was organized and released. It covered all the branches and territories of the country, and once it was concluded, the assembly process began; it included almost 3.5 million workers in more than 80,000 union sections, and more than 158,000 peasants, convened by the National Association of Small Farmers, and more than 300,000 students, in meetings organized by the Union of Young Communists.

The objectives and general principles by which the workers and their union representatives would be guided in this process would be derived from the objective analysis of the problem in each specific place as part of the country's situation and the path to be followed to reverse it.

The preparation and development of each workers' parliament required trade union leaders to assume without hesitation their roles as revolutionary activists and leaders capable of giving opinions, informing, and explaining to the workers the crucial moment that the Revolution was experiencing. In addition, they would consider what should be done in the workplace. What actions could be taken to stimulate discipline and work morale? How can production be increased and improved at lower cost? Where would it be necessary to reorganize personnel? What policy would be followed with the surplus money in circulation? What could be done to reduce or eliminate state subsidies?

It was a matter of principle that union leaders had the duty to promote the democratic participation of the workers in understanding and solving the problems affecting the functioning of each workplace. A key concern was financial reorganization. How to handle excess monetary circulation? How to solve the budget deficit? Should currency

52   HOW THE WORKERS' PARLIAMENTS

of dubious origin accumulated in large amounts by small sectors of the population be confiscated or not? What free services should be maintained and which could be eliminated? To what extent should unprofitable companies be subsidized? What role should prices play? Is it appropriate to have a tax system that taxes wages?

THE WORKERS ARE THE OWNERS

A fundamental principle of the workers' parliaments was that the workers are the owners. Therefore, solutions should be based on labor consensus. Such agreement among workers can advance plans, affirm successful ideas, and confirm the value of what has been thought and decided.

Thus, from the first discussions, the causes of economic inefficiency were examined from each labor center's perspective. These discussions also tackled the incidence of financial imbalances and offered formulations to combine the economic and the political in the course that the country should follow.

It became evident that there were no ways to increase economic efficiency other than reducing costs, increasing labor productivity, and extracting the maximum yields from the existing inputs. It was not a matter of waiting for external measures to be imposed but rather to adopt then and there those that could be implemented to make the country's economy more efficient. There were few financial proposals that did not reveal contradictions, apparent and real, of interests or conflicting criteria. For example, when one worker suggested raising the prices of certain products or charging for certain services, another reminded him that many jobs paid low wages. Another argued that it would be better to increase certain subsidized items that could be paid for by the family budget, rather than charge for vital services such as education and health, which are difficult to afford individually.

When someone thought it was better to subsidize low-income people than products sold at below cost, there was no shortage of arguments about how difficult and complex such subsidy mechanisms would be.

Among the workers' concerns were the intolerable presence of

SAVED THE CUBAN REVOLUTION 53

crime, its relationship with the black market, and its impact on labor and social discipline. There was no lack of suggestions for how to stop the thefts and diversions that raised costs, demoralized the collectives, and enriched traffickers. There was also a demand for drastic measures by the authorities at all levels to set an example.

The workers also discussed the need to comply with financial rules for collections and payments among companies, the current state of which caused indiscipline, to the extent of covering up crimes.

A LIGHT AT THE END OF THE TUNNEL

Because of all that was being done, 1994 would show signs of economic recovery. A faint light began to appear at the end of the tunnel. That year the decline was reversed, and a modest GDP growth of .70 percent was achieved. This trend continued in the following years.

There was a general recognition in the workers' parliaments of the wisdom of the National Assembly of People's Power to postpone decisions on the burning issues of economic readjustment until the democratic debate about them had taken place. Such readjustment would be done in "the Cuban way, the Fidelist way," with socialist formulas and with the majority approval of the workers.

The CTC insisted on the importance of extending and improving this democratic and educational process. All workplace administrations had to make available the information to diagnose the economic and financial condition of each workplace.

UNEQUIVOCAL SUPPORT

From the very first, the workers' parliaments enjoyed the unequivocal support of the Communist Party and the Union of Young Communists (Unión de Jóvenes Comunistas/UJC) of its leadership structures and grassroots organizations. From the preparatory meetings and the first experimental meetings in the selected workplaces that served as teaching laboratories for those tasked with leading the process at the base, to the more than 80,000 parliaments, not only the leading cadres of the national CTC participated but also the president of the National Assembly of People's Power, Ricardo Alarcón de Quesada, as well as other officials of the National Assembly and the municipal and provincial assemblies. Members of the Political Bureau and the Secretariat also met with workers' parliaments throughout the country, as well as officials from the different departments of the Central Committee of the Party and provincial and municipal Party officials. The parliaments also saw the participation of nearly all of Cuba's institutions: government ministers, officers of the armed forces and the Ministry of the Interior; the National Association of Small Farmers; the Federation of Cuban Women; the Association of Combatants of the Cuban Revolution; the National Association of Economists; the National Association of Jurists; the Union of Writers and Artists; and the Union of Journalists.

SOCIOPOLITICAL AND OPINION STUDIES:
THE FIRST SURVEY

On the eve of the massive parliament process, a team from the Center for Sociopolitical and Opinion Studies surveyed 1,306 workers from all sectors and labor categories. The survey found that 86 percent of respondents considered the process "worthwhile," 75 percent expected "useful proposals to be made," and 62 percent believed "that the idea of this parliament has generated enthusiasm."

When asked how to implement the measures that are approved, 58 percent said "gradually."

As for possible solutions, there was strong agreement about applying economic efficiency criteria and consequently reducing the number of employees; eliminating non-core costs; closing unproductive centers and implementing a wide range of monetary, financial, price, and other measures.

The study authors noted that the pilot sessions of the workers' parliament paid considerable attention to the issue of achieving greater economic efficiency. The survey found that there were also doubts and concerns. What was most troubling was the fate of the surplus workers who might be left out by a reorganization of the workforce. There were also concerns about problems related to speculation and illicit enrichment, the situation of lower-income individuals and families, and incentives to work.

But overall, optimism prevailed.

A VAST SCHOOL OF ECONOMICS

For forty-five days, Cuba became a vast school of economics and politics where much was learned. The press played an important role, contributing sound, convincing arguments, and reflections on the debate taking place throughout the country, especially in *Trabajadores*, whose message helped from the days before the beginning of the process. Radio and television also provided continuous coverage, offering critical perspectives. One of the most remarkable aspects of this period was the altruistic response of Cuban workers to the delicate and complex problem of staff reorganization and relocation. Even though they knew that the issue could affect them personally, many did not hesitate to propose and support such decisions. They placed the interests of the country—the improvement of labor productivity, cost reduction, and efficient organization of production—above their own. It was an expression of confidence that the Revolution would find just solutions.

As the development of the workers' parliaments progressed, consolidation of internal finances increasingly became a focus of the debates. There were divergent views about the basket of free services, which should be defined as essential, and prices and taxes. Different perspectives notwithstanding, there was a collective understanding that the reorganization of internal finances was an unavoidable necessity.

Another fundamental position was that any proposals regarding education and health care must protect these two pillars of the Cuban Revolution.

THE ISSUE OF PRICES

In the parliaments, discussions explored various options for using prices to remove excess currency from circulation. These included price hikes for transportation, gasoline, lubricants, and accessories; eliminating alcoholic beverages, cigars, and tobacco from the state supply list and offering them for sale in hard currency; analyzing prices in the gastronomic network and in workers' dining halls, as well as establishing water charges, and raising electricity rates and the cost of telephone services, provided those services were improved.

Although some spoke in favor of taxing wages, the prevailing opinion rejected this approach. On numerous occasions, subsidizing low-income families was proposed to protect them before price increases were implemented.

Other proposals concerned a change of currency, the confiscation of money and resources of dubious origin in the face of evident facts of illicit enrichment, the need to review and revise the Criminal Code, and more severe sanctions for crimes.

The CTC leadership guided the process by working with a group of prominent journalists. Under the leadership of the workers' union's general secretary, they prepared analytical materials every Monday for the two months in which the parliaments were being developed. Their analyses were published in *Trabajadores,* ensuring that they reached every union chapter in the country's farthest reaches.

Each week the journalists focused on a different topic. They reported important debates, highlighted the positive aspects, and pointed out problems. These journalistic analyses undoubtedly played an important role in illuminating the development and functioning of the workers' parliaments for readers.

REDUCING EMPLOYMENT ROLLS ... BUT HOW?

The results of the first 267 assemblies revealed a growing popular awareness of the need to end inflated employment rolls. However, there was no consensus concerning the tactical approach to a solution.

Downsizing was a priority, but it was not the only issue, nor, in many workplaces, the most pertinent one. Too much attention to it could distract from discussion of other matters that had greater impact on

SAVED THE CUBAN REVOLUTION 57

workplace inefficiency and which could be solved quicker and without consultations. From the beginning, there was the intention that labor reorganization should be accelerated in those workplaces where production or services were fundamental for the revival of the economy.

The January 29, 1994, plenary of the National Committee of the CTC gave direction to the workers' movement. It involved leaders from the entire CTC, including general secretaries of the trade union bureaus as well as guests of the Party, the government, and the National Assembly of People's Power. The meeting dealt with such critical topics as the reorganization of agriculture, the sugarcane industry, and the restructuring of the national economy.

There were many attempts to explain away the problems. Tourism drivers attributed part of the reduction in their income to the licenses granted to freelance taxi drivers, diverting earnings that should go into their own pockets. Aquaculture centers blamed poachers operating in the dams for the decrease in their own captures, failing to assume responsibility for their lack of diligence in the workplace.

But when the debate deepened on those and many other issues, it was made evident that things were not that simple and that, often, there was a "beam" in their very own eyes that did not let people see the actual causes of the problems manifested.

We knew, of course, that the difficulties were of a different nature and that false expectations were not to be encouraged. The lack of foreign currency, oil, raw materials, and other resources to boost production meant that we had to make better use of what we had. The discussion highlighted that there was no need to go far to discover everything that could be extracted in an environment of order, discipline, and honesty—sometimes the reserves were right there, within reach of workers. We insisted that the workers' parliaments were not celebratory or decorative; people knew how conditions were and we had to look inward. If we could not demonstrate the capacity to tackle our problems, there was little chance we could legislate solutions affecting the entire country.

The plenary also warned about the need not to run marathons or senseless races to solve problems. It also brought to light the peril that

58   HOW THE WORKERS' PARLIAMENTS

some workers might think they had been called to the meetings only to
confirm preestablished criteria. The reality was that everyone was there
to be consultants on the measures we should implement. Workers were
asked to speak out, express their thoughts, reflect, offer arguments,
seek truth—all together. If we worked that way, it would be impossible
not to move forward.

OUR MEETING WITH THE CIGAR WORKERS' PARLIAMENT

Our responsibility was to manage the process of workers, keeping in
daily contact with the Commander in Chief, who consistently demonstrated his interest in what was being discussed—the opinions
expressed, the main proposals, and the outlook of the workers. We
took part in seventy-nine workers' parliaments in centers representative of all the sectors of the economy—services, education, public
health, science, culture, and sports—in all the provinces and the
Special Municipality of Isla de la Juventud.[14]

In a workers' parliament convened at a major cigar factory in Havana,
we encountered discontent among workers over the many difficulties
they were facing. And once again, we heard workers lay the blame for
their problems outside the factory.

Thus it was necessary to address a misunderstanding regarding an
investment of 50 million in foreign currency in the construction of a
high-technology scientific facility that few First World nations had.
This, at a time when the country required so many basic things.

This was not an issue appropriate for the cigar workers' parliament
because it did not pertain to their workplace or economic sector. We
explained exactly what the investment in a scientific center with state-
of-the-art technology meant strategically for the development of the
country and the welfare of the population. We left feeling certain that
the workers understood this issue.

Sounding out what was happening in the factory itself, we found
that the working conditions were unsuitable, a condition that was
reproduced in other industries of the sector. For example, the lighting was insufficient for cigar production. The necessary tools—rolling

boards, flick-knives, vises, molds, and the fixtures to decorate the cigar boxes—were missing or damaged. The raw material was of low quality. The majority of the workers lived in the outskirts of Havana, in the Alamar neighborhood, which, given the transportation problems, meant that they arrived at work late, or not at all, given the high rate of absenteeism. In addition, the food for the workers' cafeteria was supplied by trading cigars with other entities.

The cigar export plan for that year was only 35 million units, which had a negative impact on both the economy and workers' salaries because this production level required only fifteen workdays per month.

Among other concerns the workers expressed was that hotels near the factory were selling products not included in the state market basket, such as the asthma drug salbutamol, which could not be found in state pharmacies, and required payment in foreign currency.

Our meeting was held in the part of the factory where cigars were twisted and finished. One employee of another area had traversed the three floors of the factory several times, awaiting her turn to address the meeting. Given the atmosphere of baring grievances, we wondered what the worker might say. She began by saying that she was asthmatic, but that was not what she was going to talk about. Then she said, "What I want to say here is that the only Revolution that gives bread for five cents every day to each kid and each citizen, is ours!" At that moment, the sound of the workers banging flick-knives on their work tables—which is how cigar makers applaud—filled the room. In a difficult moment, the worker's words roused the collective, and from that moment on, we were immersed in the real work of the parliament, identifying the problems and analyzing possible solutions.

Then, we took the floor and asked, "What is the source of the cigars that are being sold in the flea market of the Boulevard? What is the source of the fixtures, the boxes, the bands, the raw material—everything? How much raw material is lost in production?"

The managers who accompanied me and the director of the factory answered that the loss rate estimated for that year was 3 percent. Then,

60 HOW THE WORKERS' PARLIAMENTS

we asked how the loss rate of the factory was doing. They told us that it was between 18 and 21 percent. Someone said that the raw material was of poor quality. We wanted to know what they did with the scraps, which would have to be substantial.

We assumed that the cigars offered to tourists in the streets, with their boxes and falsified brands, would have to be coming from the raw materials supposedly being set aside in the factory but actually were being removed from the factory's production. We agreed to return to the factory to continue the discussion of these issues.

KEEPING FIDEL INFORMED

We tried to contact the Commander in Chief to inform him about the problem that the cigar makers' parliament raised about the sale of medication in foreign currencies in the hotels. We recounted the discussion to one of his aides. At midnight, our office telephone rang and we received Fidel Castro's response: tell the workers that medications would no longer be sold in hotels in foreign currency.

We returned the next day to the factory with the news, which the workers received enthusiastically. When the parliament resumed, we determined that the cigars being sold to tourists indeed did come from the factory itself. We now addressed the problems related to factory lighting, tools, and the workers' transportation.

But that wasn't all. We adopted changes in all factories producing cigars for export. Through our participation in the parliament, we learned that the workers had been experiencing problems even before the Special Period, and that they had worsened over the past five years.

Workers spoke of the dismantling in 1976 of the integration of aspects of production and marketing in Cuba's planned economy. They noted the loss of quality control, the tendency toward bureaucratic mentalities, and the uncontrolled growth of entrepreneurialism.

We, on behalf of the CTC, spoke about the structural problems the workers identified. Factories employed a transportation director despite having only one truck, and even that one often was nonfunctional. There was excessive dead weight in management personnel,

SAVED THE CUBAN REVOLUTION   61

rigidity in price mechanisms, impediments to directors trying to make adjustments to salaries. For example, there was a payment to certain workers for every thousand cigars that was not available to other crucial workers in the industry. During discussion of the workers' transportation issue, the point was made that using just one bus to guarantee punctual attendance would represent the production of 5,000 cigars more each day, equivalent to the same amount of dollars.

Minister of Agriculture Alfredo Jordán concurred that there needed to be a return to an integrated process of cigar production and marketing, from the tobacco fields to export.

The meeting concluded with the president of the National Assembly of People's Power, Ricardo Alarcón, who stressed the validity of the workers' parliament process and the results it was producing. In 1994, Cuba exceeded its planned cigar production by 10 million. From then on, production grew, until reaching 200 million cigars for export.

WITH THE MILKMEN IN PINAR DEL RÍO

Ricardo Alarcón also accompanied us to the meeting of another workers' parliament, in a livestock company in Pinar del Río province. The meeting, which lasted more than five hours, began with an in-depth discussion of the reliability of production reports. We also discussed whether to eliminate or reduce the subsidy to milk production. It cost 72 cents to produce one liter of milk; the company was paid 37 cents per liter, and each unit was sold to the public at 25 cents.

The issue was how to lower production costs in the agriculture sector, where losses, in 1993, reached 300 million pesos in Pinar del Río. By reducing costs and increasing productivity, losses would be reduced. The workers expressed their belief that "the population needs to be educated that the state is not responsible for meeting all individual needs," and that "the budget should not be augmented from any one single source but from the small and many contributions each entity must provide."

How to handle the problem of redundancy in the workforce was

62 HOW THE WORKERS' PARLIAMENTS

another key issue. They were missing people in the production, while "the offices were crawling with employees."

Ricardo Alarcón stated that our People's Power system had to consolidate itself in reaching the people, not in a rhetorical sense but in each workplace. "We can do that by mobilizing labor collectives," he said. "Coming here to discuss this with you already demonstrates our confidence in the people, in the workers."

WORKERS' PARLIAMENTS IN CAMAGÜEY

We began meetings at the University of Camagüey, the first to be established after the Revolution triumphed. "I was an absentee," confessed a worker at the university cafeteria, and the assembly livened with murmurs. "I live far away. Today, I had to get here on foot, and, hey, with how transport is . . . I get complacent . . ."

More problems began to surface in the workers' parliament. Cafeteria workers mentioned that because of a lack of detergent they used sand and ashes to wash casseroles and trays.

Absenteeism, as in many places, was a serious problem as well, reaching 16 percent. Workers were presenting more than 100 notes per month from physicians excusing them from work. The ethical responsibility of physicians was a genuine issue. Salaries, however, were low, which affected the motivation to work. Exigencies of daily life also contributed to the high rate of absenteeism.

With respect to the problem of the food supply, there was a proposal to mobilize forty workers for one year to a site where food production would be for the university cafeteria. Doubts were expressed about this idea. Some brought up previous experiences of this sort, of people earning 16 pesos per day who nonetheless barely worked a full two hours. However, a staff member of the university's department of veterinary medicine said that its faculty could provide enough people for the project. What was lacking was not staff but clear, precise ideas about how to proceed..

The assembled workers applauded these comments. After this discussion, we invited them to create a model farm operated efficiently and with a well-studied program. We encouraged them to get involved in that adventure if they wanted to have a better cafeteria. By the end of the meeting, a new, enthusiastic spirit had emerged.

THE WORKERS' PARLIAMENT AT THE LENIN
CENTRAL WORKSHOP

That afternoon, we participated in the workers' parliament at the Lenin Central Workshop, where combine harvester engines for sugarcane were repaired. There, absenteeism was 11 percent. Workers spoke about their efforts to reduce it, noting that a physician who had been providing false medical excuses to workers had been fired from the plant.

We explained to them that the rate of absenteeism from the workshop was equivalent to forty-five days not worked, which, with vacation time, meant that the workshop was productive for only nine months per year. The quality of work at the plant also was a problem. Eleven percent of engines that had been repaired were rejected, rendering useless 204 combine harvesters. As one worker stressed, no one was held accountable.

We noted what those defective repairs meant for the sugarcane harvest. For example, if a UBPC (Basic Unit of Cooperative Production), in which five combine harvesters were used to chop reeds, received only two of those engines, reed chopping would be reduced by 40 percent.

We asked the workers if they felt they could preserve the status of "Labor Exploit" (an honorary award) that they had earned the previous year for having repaired 600 engines in two months. "We are a collective that knows how to do our duty," they replied, their pride evident. They proposed to put the engines through the test bed to detect and fix any defects.

Food for the workers' cafeteria was another pressing concern. We proposed to create an organoponic garden near the workshop with the redundant employees. An older man vigorously demanded the opportunity to join the agricultural project, despite his age. At the end, solutions of two major problems, food and downsizing, had emerged from our discussion with the workers.

But the story did not end there. On March 28, 1994, *Trabajadores* published the following article: "Let's Name it 'Ignacio Agramonte.'"

Ilsa, a good-natured and eloquent speaker who leaves nothing unspoken when it comes to her workplace, dropped a bomb in the rigid ritualism that still haunts us like a bad shadow.

The workers of the Lenin Workshops fulfilled the commitment set in the parliament by repairing, in February, 252 engines, more than the 250 committed. They earned, fair and square, the right to receive the flag acknowledging their accomplishments from the hands of the Secretary of the Provincial Party, Julián Rizo, and Pedro Ross. They had fulfilled 10 of the 25 commitments agreed upon in that forum.

She spoke about personal consumption: the workers' cafeteria is fine, but what about at home? Ilsa, seated in the first row, kicked off a discussion that soon became a debate.

"Do you know how many acres of m*arabú*[15] there are in Camagüey?" Rizo asked. Some figures were thrown out: Thirty-seven? Fifty-six? "No, there are almost 690. We need to know about m*arabú* but above all, we need quick action."

"Here, a model Basic Unit of Cooperative Production can be established," Ross proposed. "Shall we wait until next year when we might do it today? Our homes and families wait for food and here there are 610 workers; you could take 100 and the rest would guarantee production. The first two years will be for promotion and personal consumption; then, contributions to the economy could be made. This could become an example for all the workplaces and for the labor movement."

"We will give you 14 acres," Rizo said, "and cows and hens."

"But there needs to be greater labor discipline," Ross said. "That's one of the conditions for having the UBPC. Absenteeism has reached 8 percent; it has to be reduced to 3 percent. Otherwise, you won't receive the National Vanguard honor."

The workers committed to repairing 255 additional combine

SAVED THE CUBAN REVOLUTION   65

harvester engines by April. These are crucial to the sugarcane harvest. The parliament will continue, and in May, we will return to assess this commitment and the UBPC's performance.

Do we agree? There is a vote. People agree. Approved. There is jubilation in the air. Ilsa laughs and keeps talking.

"It will be necessary to talk with the labor leaders of the province and to infect them with this drive to carry on a fight against marabou. And what should we call the UBPC?"

Some names were proposed, but Ross said, "Let's name it Ignacio Agramonte because you know what he answered when asked what he counted on to continue the war for independence from Spain: With the dignity of the Cubans!"[16]

A March 28, 1994, article in *Trabajadores* by the journalist Julio García Luis summarized one of our visits to nine provinces and the Special Municipality of Isla de la Juventud. The following is an excerpt from Garcia's article.

The territorial assessment meetings of the workers' parliaments in nine provinces and the Special Municipality of Isla de la Juventud were completed last week. Tens of thousands of concrete measures are being carried out. But most significant is the workers' determination to persist and their desire for new approaches and novel thinking to take root.

In the main hall of the provincial government, the people of Cienfuegos hung a large painting depicting the Mal Tiempo battle.[17] Behind fences, the Spanish troops fight to maintain their defense, while [Maximo] Gómez, [Antonio] Maceo, and [Serafín] Sánchez, waving their machetes, throw themselves onto the troops, leading the three forces that decided the outcome of that bloody encounter. In the background, sugarcane plantations burn.

Perhaps unintentionally they have represented two crucial emblems of the province and of the country in the current situation: cooperation and drive.

Last week, in a marathon that seemed endless, I accompanied

Pedro Ross to the assessment meetings in nine provinces, which became, in turn, the same number of workers' parliaments. Everywhere, the painting of the Mal Tiempo battle came back to me: the country has taken the offensive and, at the cost of sacrifice and suffering, is turning the situation around.

WITH FIDEL: SALARY GUARANTEE AND OTHER TOPICS

In one of our meetings with Fidel (always held at night), we analyzed the vexing problem of the guaranteed salaries of workers in enterprises in which activities were being interrupted. He had previously raised this issue with us. The CTC offered its criteria and proposals, as well as the Ministry of Labor (MINTRAB), whose main official, Francisco "Panchito" Linares Calvo, also would participate in that exchange.

First, Fidel received our information about how things were developing and then gave Panchito the opportunity to address the topic he wanted to discuss with us.

MINTRAB had produced a technical document with three classifications of potential redundant workers and the salary guarantee that would correspond to each one of those three groups, based on seniority, with a maximum equivalent of 60 percent of the salary for those who had worked the longest. CTC's proposal amounted to 75 percent.

Based on the information we in the CTC and MINTRAB presented, Fidel raised the salary guarantee to 80 percent and increased the duration of the guarantee. He was very interested in our proposal to mobilize redundant workers to workplaces that needed large workforces that could make the enterprises profitable—for example, in sugarcane and other crops.

These kinds of great mobilizations were not unprecedented; they had been utilized in agriculture in the mid-1980s. Sugarcane was the only crop that needed more than 100,000 additional workers for the sowing, cultivation, and harvesting of the cane.

The pressing issue was how to produce food under existing conditions. Many entities requested and took on agricultural areas that were unproductive because they lacked workers. CTC set up a farm in the Pedro Pí zone near the freeway, which was overrun with m*arabú*. We named it La Tacita (the Little Cup). After five years, our Little Cup was overflowing; today, it still yields agricultural products for the CTC, producing with economic efficiency. All officers, functionaries, and CTC workers participated in this endeavor.

Fidel had encouraged the formation of agricultural and construction contingents—as did Raúl Castro—to mobilize the nation, under the slogan, "Yes, it is possible" (or "Yes, we can). He gave the highest priority to mobilizing and relocating workers for the vital production of food and sugarcane.

The salary documents, with the maximum percent set by Fidel Castro, were approved and published, as were measures to maximize the relocation of redundant workers toward the productive activities of agriculture and construction. The latter sector, instead of being paralyzed because of the restrictions of the Special Period, was invigorated with the building of hotels and the tourism infrastructure.

One example of this was the Lenin Contingent, created with the personal presence of Fidel. He explained thoroughly to the workers that after construction of the Juragua nuclear power plant was suspended in Cienfuegos[18] they should focus on other priorities, such as hotels, in order to obtain much-needed foreign currency, as well as engineering projects in the tourist sector, in Varadero.[19]

THE BUILDING CONTRACTOR CONTINGENTS

During 1994, one of our highest priorities (along with the establishment and development of the labor parliaments) was the building contractor contingents, a mechanism to boost productivity in high-priority works. One of these was the construction of the East-West Freeway. As Pedro Chávez González, then president of the People's Power Provincial Assembly of Havana, put it, "For the construction of the East-West Freeway, there was a project of eight kilometers. We were told to select the personnel and a chief for this brigade, which would be subordinated to the capital government.... Once this matter

68 HOW THE WORKERS' PARLIAMENTS

was solved, we felt that we were ready to constitute the brigade, headed by comrade Cándido Palmero."

Blas Roca Calderío, the First Contingent

Fidel Castro decided to create the first building contractor contingent, naming it for the late Blas Roca Calderío.[20] After that first contingent, others were organized, eventually totaling seventy nationwide. These incorporated 27 percent of workers from the Ministry of Construction and produced more than the 60 percent of the value generated in this sector. The contingents played a crucial role in the Special Period, in hotel construction—including the majestic Cohíba Hotel in Havana—and tourism-related infrastructure projects. They also created new airports and extended existing ones and built causeways and hydraulic plants.

The Miguel Enríquez Hospital Contingent

The Sixth Congress contingent was created to build the Miguel Enríquez Hospital in Havana. More than 40,000 square meters (nearly ten acres) were to be built. This major work required architects, technicians, engineers, and specialists of all the branches of construction.

Fidel established that this work had to be completed in one year—"neither one day more, nor one day less"—and that we were to find the technical force for it in the ministries of Construction and Industry. We began to comply with his mandate by convening an assembly with the MICONS (Ministry of Construction) collective. We explained the importance of the hospital project and informed them that Fidel had said that the construction ministry should provide most of the workers for it. More than 400 workers expressed their willingness to participate. So there, on the happy afternoon of October 19, 1987 (which also was my forty-eighth birthday), we created the Miguel Enríquez Hospital Contingent.

Fidel consistently demonstrated his commitment to the project. He would visit the construction site at any time of day, at night or early in the morning, sometimes accompanied by foreign visitors. His involvement even extended to the food he had provided to the contingent: he would have lunch and dinner with the workers, after first stopping in the kitchen to inspect the meals. He also visited the workers in their living quarters.

And as he requested, the hospital was built within a year, with the contingent putting in twenty-four hour workdays. This extraordinary experience was repeated in other important works undertaken by the building contractor contingents.

EXCHANGING IDEAS WITH FIDEL

We were in constant communication with the Commander in Chief, discussing with him the development of the workers' parliaments, the problems that were emerging, and their solutions. Issues that we discussed included implementing the legalization of foreign currency, which was necessary because the only alternative would be to confiscate dollars circulating in the country. Other matters discussed were:

- New taxation systems
- Reducing expenses and especially loss subsidies
- The elimination of wrongful subsidies
- Higher electricity and telephone rates
- The organization of work and the structure of salaries
- The need for greater labor efficiency, discipline, and productivity, and for reduced production costs
- The need to identify and confront negative distortions and tendencies
- Inflated staff rolls
- The proper management of freelance work
- Creation of new basic units of cooperative production
- Stockpiling and distribution of agricultural and livestock products
- Self-financing of artistic creation
- Price increases for non-essential products
- Severe penalties for persons who illicitly enriched themselves, including those who diverted state resources

- Charging a fee for citizens' identity cards
- Increasing interest rates paid by banks to promote saving accounts among the Cuban people
- Improved expenditure control and audit procedures
- Following the example the armed forces had set in conservation and rational use of resources, their self-sufficiency and contributions of food for the population
- The need to preserve emblematic universally free services, like public health and education, as symbols
- The need to counter harmful generalizations—about Cuba being full of "*macetas*" (black market hustlers who illegally buy and sell goods such as food, clothes, liquor), young women prowling hotels to sell sex to tourists, and children begging for money. These were real problems but they were not typical of Cuban society.
- The need for the Cuban people to take the initiative in identifying the nation's problems and their solutions
- The recognition that so-called existing socialism failed because it had abandoned the Marxist principle, "From each according to one's ability, to each according to one's needs."
- The role of the press in this process, aiming to improve its work
- A currency change would be counterproductive, even if applied after eliminating the causes of the excess money supply.
- The policy of subsidizing people and not products
- Mobilizing redundant workers to organoponics
- Charging for cultural activities
- Increasing revenue from rum and cigar sales
- The need for the state to analyze factories in terms of their costs, efficiency, and profitability. In ascertaining why some factories are profitable and others not, objective and subjective factors must be considered.
- Workers and trade unions should not leave the solutions to problems to highly educated experts. All workers should know the problems of their workplaces, such as the causes of unprofitability, to be able to correct them.
- The need to revise the policies of the credits being granted

SAVED THE CUBAN REVOLUTION 71

- The need to analyze, with political sense, the criteria of specialists, and that the best economists are those capable of elaborating measures with political sense

In all our political and ideological discussions, we were guided by the spirit of January 1, 1959. These ideas, and many others the Commander in Chief exchanged with us, were also taken up in the workers' parliament debates.

ANOTHER SURVEY: WORKERS ENDORSE
THE PARLIAMENTS

In February 1994, the Center of Sociopolitical and Opinion Studies conducted a second survey to sound out Cuban opinions of the economic transformations then underway.

Sixty-two percent of respondents to the first survey, conducted in January, were enthusiastic about the debates occurring in workers' parliaments all over the country. One month later, that figure rose to 80 percent. In January, 75 percent felt the parliaments would produce useful proposals to increase efficiency and reorganize the finances of the country; in February, the figure rose to 85 percent. After thousands of parliaments were held throughout Cuba, another poll conducted in March found that these indicators—enthusiasm for the workers' parliaments process and confidence that they would produce useful proposals—had increased to 86 then 91 percent.

Surveys found that public opinion about price policy changes had evolved. In October 1993, 68 percent of workers favored changes in price policy as a potential measure to reverse the country's economic crisis. In February, this figure reached 74 percent. (However, consensus was elusive when it came to price changes for specific products or services.)

In the last survey, 50 percent supported increasing prices of alcoholic drinks; 45 percent favored price increases for cigars. Sixty percent favored raising electricity rates.

How to increase economic efficiency had been the dominant topic

72 HOW THE WORKERS' PARLIAMENTS

during the workers' parliament debates. A study of the debates found that there were many more opinions about this issue than about the reorganization of domestic finances.

A growing awareness of the need for increased and more efficient production was reflected in surveys conducted in October 1993 and February 1994. Only a minority of workers opposed reducing inflated employment rolls and closing unproductive workplaces.

There was a decrease over the same period in support for maintaining subsidies for products guaranteed by the ration book distribution system. On the other hand, the potential elimination of non-fundamental subsidies gained the approval of 71 percent of those polled.

That a majority support did not exist when it came to the introduction of taxes was a logical reflection of the absence, for years and with some exceptions, of tax policy.

The new opinion survey reiterated a well-defined group of issues: the future of redundant workers, the commitment of the low-income workers, the enrichment of the "*macetas,*" and the effectiveness of the economic measures being applied. These issues reflected the pervasive support for the Revolution's ideals of equality and social justice.

A vital subject addressed both in the parliaments and in the assessment meetings of the CTC held in each province was the inflated staff rolls, the relocation of redundant workers, the loss of qualified workforces, and the weight of bureaucracy. Also, in addressing such sensitive problems, it was stressed that the search for solutions must not cause the abandonment of any worker.

ASSESSMENT TIME: WHAT HAPPENED IN THE PARLIAMENTS?

On March 29, 1994, the National Commission of the CTC assessed the performance of the workers' parliaments. Fidel Castro participated in the meeting, along with fourteen members of both the Politburo and the entire government.

We opened the meeting by presenting a report on behalf of the leadership of the CTC. We analyzed the results of the recently concluded

SAVED THE CUBAN REVOLUTION 73

workers' parliaments, in which more than three million workers discussed the problems of their workplaces. The parliaments also produced an inventory of measures to reorganize domestic finances. The workers demonstrated the will and commitment to do whatever was necessary to preserve the Revolution.

We also presented a summary of the main items discussed in the parliaments, organized into two core topics: economic efficiency and reorganization of domestic finances.

The presence of Fidel and such a large representation of the nation's highest leadership might have suggested that the meeting's purpose was to receive information. What prevailed, however, was in the best spirit of the parliaments. Every statement was received with interest, ideas were exchanged, concepts were clarified, and the most important agreements that emerged from the vast national debate were noted. As the discussion proceeded it became increasingly evident that all the country's problems were interrelated.

Everyone saw how the parliaments shook up the labor collectives, promoted solutions and palliative measures for many problems, augmented the labor initiatives and the capability of administrative management. The parliaments contributed to the formulation of medium- and long-term national strategies. But we were also aware that the debates themselves would not provide the six million tons of oil we needed, nor could it refund the 75 percent we had lost when imports were abruptly cut off.

Fidel told us to not think that goodwill was sufficient to solve all our problems. He offered the example of the country's need to gather a minimum amount of foreign currency. The state, he said, was the sole owner of the shops that sold products at high prices in dollars to recover some needed foreign currency. He noted that some items could not be traded in dollars, like medications, which were lacking because of a misguided initiative by businessmen and not caused by the Ministry of Public Health.

One of the climactic moments of the plenary was the analysis of workplace problems. They were the result of inflated staff rolls, the temporary relocation of workers, the loss of qualified personnel, and

74 HOW THE WORKERS' PARLIAMENTS

the de-bureaucratization of burdensome technical and administrative machinery. That discussion made it evident to all that if these issues were not addressed it would not be possible to achieve economic efficiency or reorganize domestic finances.

The problem, though, was that our depressed and contracted economy reduced our options for a quick reorganization of the Cuban labor army. In this respect, we looked to the experience of the nickel industry, where we identified excess personnel without waiting for the problem to arise in negotiations with foreign capital.

Minister of Labor Francisco Linares insisted on taking into account the actual conditions of the country. We could not guarantee that all relocated workers would be assigned to good and productive positions. He also pointed out that some provinces were more able than others to mobilize workers in agriculture and other sectors experiencing labor deficits. Linares also stated that the trade unions, with their political and oversight work, played an essential role. He referred to the enormous economic burden on the state, noting that reduced subsidies were necessary to lighten the load. Linares added that the Revolution must prevent the "de-proletarianizing" of the working class, the weakening of the workers' collectives.

Not everything said in the meeting was valuable. There were some unwarranted apologetics on behalf of some economic sectors, as well as some self-indulgent comments, which, though not detracting from the generally positive atmosphere of the plenary, wasted valuable time. In contrast, there were testimonies like those of Rafael Stuart, a trade union leader in Cienfuegos, who spoke of the tremendous daily struggles of workers in the electric power sector, and that of the welders of the Carlos Manuel de Céspedes thermoelectric facility. Workers at the facility—who had enjoyed National Vanguard status for several years— would repair breakdowns before the boilers' air preheaters had cooled down. Marcia Cobas, from the Sciences Trade Union of Havana, spoke about erroneous concepts of self-sufficiency that she had to refute in her sector's parliament. The role of science, she asserted, was not just to finance itself but the country.

The debate reached consensus about the validity of the workers' parliament approach. It promoted the active participation of workers in analyzing Cuba's problems. The parliaments put at the country's disposal an army of ideas and proposals to reorganize domestic finances and achieve economic efficiency. The parliaments attested to the importance of frank, critical, and self-critical analysis.

A FAINT RAY OF LIGHT

Fidel Castro said that we should feel proud of our successes in meeting the tests we faced, and that a faint ray of light was becoming visible. Indeed, pride and certainty emanated from that extended plenary of the CTC. We were moved by the fact that we could face such complex problems with solidarity and sensitivity, and that we would move forward with majority support for the measures that had to be implemented. We had generated ideas that would guide our work for years to come.

The Commander in Chief also noted:

- We need to increase national production to substitute imports based on their commercialization in the foreign currency market.
- People should not be sent home (or simply made redundant); this would, inevitably, create negative financial imbalances.
- Because of the situation generated by the Special Period, the financial imbalance it caused entailed a devaluation of the Cuban peso and the introduction of the dollar. If visitors to Cuba bring dollars, they are welcome because they will be spent in Cuba. The bitter price of inequality and privilege upsets us, but it is conditioned by the need, imposed by reality, to raise foreign currency.
- Profitability is associated with economic efficiency. This is linked to the inflated staffing issue.
- Local industry in the cities has to be strengthened to address the problem of excess currency and as a source of employment.
- Economic activity that generates substantial revenue must be linked to a graduated taxation system.
- National production to be traded on the foreign currency market

carries the condition of generating profits, of being produced at the same cost and with the same consumption of electricity as if they were imported. Many products are more conveniently made here and this must be encouraged to collect foreign currency.

- Indiscipline in the collection and payment of accounts must be eliminated.
- One peso is not actually worth one cent because, compared with other countries, there are costs, like housing, that in many places represent 50 percent of salaries. What's the monetary value of health and education?
- Workers' parliaments have been an important step, as demonstrated by the number of subjects, problems, and solutions proposed. The process has yielded more results than expected, not only in awareness but also in efficiency. The process reflected the workers' enthusiasm for socialism and for the Revolution—the political consciousness of the working class.
- Better news about the economy is coming. The most difficult juncture has passed and we are seeing some improvements. Not much more can be expected.
- Cuba can benefit from increased production of sugarcane, tobacco, food items, vegetables, and oil, as well as income from tourism and the legalization of the dollar, exports of biotechnology products, and medications.
- The quality of education and public health is improving.
- Incentives should be offered, resources permitting. However, we should be very careful about it.
- There is no need to renounce the change of currency.
- The National Assembly will provide a set of recommendations, and the government will decide among them. Measures will not be implemented all at once but according to priorities. Some measures, however, can be implemented before the assembly (which is in session).

SAVED THE CUBAN REVOLUTION

After this fruitful, ten-hour meeting, we all felt that the Revolution was advancing to create our Cuban version of socialism. As Fidel said, "All of us have to put together the pieces of this puzzle and make it work."

So ended a process in which crucial subjects were discussed, generating ideas and proposals. The parliaments promoted solutions and palliative measures for many obstacles. They provided a space for collective analysis of the crisis the country was confronting after the collapse of the European socialist model and the reinforcement of the U.S. blockade. The parliaments also exposed our own insufficiencies—the instances of indiscipline, the lack of order and control, bureaucratic inertia, and obsolete practices that hindered innovation.

The workers' parliaments expressed the political culture of the great majority of the Cuban workers in hard times. In them, they asserted their confidence in Fidel and the Revolution, and their will to defend the Revolution's work. Participants were candid not only about the need for economic and productive transformation; they also were self-critical about their own shortcomings.

THE FINAL SUMMARY OF THE WORKERS' PARLIAMENTS

Data from the final summary of the workers' parliament discussions tell us the following:

- More than 80,000 workers' parliaments were held all over the country, with approximately 261,859 proposals discussed.
- Of the three fundamental topics discussed, the proposals in favor of a balanced budget and reorganized domestic finances accounted for 58 percent of the most important statements, followed by the proposals to increase economic efficiency (23 percent) and those related to workforce and discipline (19 percent).

The proposals presented in more than one-thousand meetings were ranked as in Table 10 (page 78):

TABLE 1

PROPOSALS	PERCENT
• Eliminate non-fundamental free services.	22
• Control, exigency, fight against offenses.	17
• Increase production.	10
• Preserve free services and subsidies.	9.0
• Establish active price policy.	7.0
• Change of currency.	6.0
• Quality of the productive process.	6.0
• Labor legislation, discipline.	6.0
• Stimulation of workers' services.	6.0
• Tax policy.	5.0
• Reorganization of the workforce.	3.0
• Standards for freelance workers.	3.0

The occurrence of proposals in more than 5,000 parliaments is as follows:

TABLE 2

STATEMENTS	NO. OF TIMES
• Confiscate illicit goods and resources from *macetas*.	14,904
• Charge for aesthetic surgeries and other elective services.	11,507
• Improve workers' services.	8,911
• Charge for recreational activities.	8,863
• Charge for sports activities.	7,631
• Increase production.	7,520
• More rational use of resources.	6,619
• Better control of resources.	6,583
• Change currency.	6,472
• Charge for cultural activities.	6,000
• No charge for education and public health.	5,217
• Deregulate cigars and moderately raise their prices.	5,035

The proposals in 3,000 to 5,000 parliaments are indicated in Table 3 (page 79). The proposals in 1,000 to 3,000 parliaments are listed in Table 4 (page 80).

A more detailed breakdown of proposals that emerged from the workers' parliaments appears in Appendix A (page 156).

TABLE 3

STATEMENTS	NO. OF TIMES
• No tax on salaries.	4,955
• Increase production of items in high demand.	3,958
• Deregulate alcoholic drinks and their prices.	3,550
• Make better use of the working day.	3,537
• Maintain the prices of essential items.	3,439
• Maintain free education.	3,318
• Charge for medical assistance for accidents and violence.	3,201
• Abolish *macetas*.	3,490
• No change to currency.	3,043

THE MINISTRY OF FINANCES AND PRICES REPORTS

After we spoke, Minister of Finances and Prices José Luis Rodríguez announced that he would present fundamental principles to guide solutions of the nation's problems. The principles reflected the workers' parliaments discussions and the opinions of officials and the Cuban people.

Rodriguez said that the principles of social justice and solidarity must prevail, and that no one would be neglected. There would be no neoliberal adjustment policies. He noted that corrective measures inevitably would entail sacrifice. In the monetary sphere, there was excess liquidity, in the financial sphere, state budgetary deficits. Balance would be found by increasing goods and services, based on increased production. But, given the impossibility of achieving the needed magnitude of growth in the short term, it was necessary to reduce demand, revalue the national currency, and increase production and services.

The initial steps of financial reorganization, the minister said, were being implemented, with agreed-upon substantial reductions of budgetary deficits.

Regarding Cuba's money supply, both national and freely convertible currency, Rodriguez stated:

As to the national currency, as of March 1994, the excess money supply amounted to 11,636 million pesos; 59 percent was deposited

TABLE 4

STATEMENTS	NO. OF TIMES
• Create a legal peasant market with state taxes and prices.	2,919
• Establish state prices for freelance workers.	2,675
• Relocate redundant personnel to prioritized works.	2,670
• Control the black market sale of medications.	2,525
• Reallocate personnel of unproductive workplaces.	2,438
• Create corps of inspectors.	2,437
• Allocate idle lands to peasants.	2,260
• Do not charge for sports activities.	2,168
• Consider an income tax for freelance work.	2,092
• Link workers and self-supply activities.	2,086
• Confirm the veracity of medical certificates.	1,991
• Demand a higher fulfillment of obligations under labor legislation.	1,938
• The Ministry of Public Health (MINSAP) issues medical certificates.	1,817
• Improve the quality of production.	1,795
• Revise the penal code.	1,690
• Pay each worker fairly for their work.	1,650
• More control of production and services.	1,613
• Charge for uniforms and study materials.	1,602
• Base prices on quality.	1,570
• Enterprises can own self-supply area.	1,568
• To revise the granting of licenses to freelance workers.	1,520
• Assess the amount of redundant personnel.	1,467
• Raise the price of electricity based on consumption.	1,409
• No increase in transportation fees.	1,396
• Deregulate cigarette sales.	1,323
• Make enterprises profitable.	1,320
• Changing currency will not solve the problem of excess money.	1,319
• Analyze the origin of the raw material used by freelance workers.	1,318
• Close unprofitable enterprises.	1,241
• Revise what is legislated regarding certificates.	1,213
• Reduce management and administrative personnel.	1,178
• Charge for water, with reasonable prices.	1,145
• To properly select the staff working in the tourist sector.	1,120
• Preserve the rationed sale of cigarettes and sell cigarettes at deregulated, reasonable prices.	1,106
• Establish a price system for freelance work.	1,103
• Distribute rum per family unit, at reasonable prices.	1,036

SAVED THE CUBAN REVOLUTION   81

in savings accounts at the Banco Popular de Ahorro, with 41percent in cash money.

During the first two to three months of the year, liquidity has continued to grow. If no measures are taken to curb this tendency, we would reach a much higher figure by the end of the year.

The primary income sources of our population show, according to the latest estimates, that 44 percent of the workers earn basic salaries of up to 148 pesos a month, while 32 percent earned between 149 and 198 pesos a month.

Also, pensions were mainly between 60 and 98 pesos, representing 62 percent of pensioners.

Low-income families represented approximately 24 percent of family units.

Income is being distributed based on the existence of freely convertible currency, which, with the legalization of foreign currency, has had an impact but has not affected the substance of many of our current realities.

Taking these premises into consideration, monetary and financial reorganization must be closely linked to the redefinition of other policies that are being adjusted, basically at the enterprise level, to achieve the greatest economic efficiency and increased production.

Monetary and financial reorganization entail coherent measures whose intended effects should be clearly defined. Those effects would be gradually felt until they have matured, probably in no less than eighteen months.

He then explained that

the measures for reducing the budgetary deficit constitute an indispensable element when evaluating the financial reorganization of the country. In the budget for 1994, the government decided to reduce this fiscal deficit by approximately one billion pesos, in the current year, which would represent a 24 percent reduction that will reduce subsidies of losses (1.3 billion pesos in the 1994 budget).

Regarding accounts receivable and accounts payable, at the end of last year, 3,899 million pesos corresponded to accounts receivable, of which more than 97percent were in the business sector.

These accounts had a 41 percent expiry date of 30 days—a normal collection period. Another 28 percent, were thirty-one to ninety days old; another 31 percent, more than ninety days.

On average, the more than 30-day accounts represented only 12.4 percent of the value of sales.

An analysis initiated by state entities and local People's Power bodies led, during the first quarter of this year, to an 11.3 percent reduction of these balances of accounts receivable, representing in round numbers 40 million pesos that remained outstanding since December 1, 1993.

On the other hand, regarding accounts receivable in freely convertible currency, there was a balance of approximately 209.8 million pesos. However, this figure—equivalent to 47.5 percent of accounts receivable—corresponded to activity in foreign currency among national entities; 52.5 percent of the total was the net balance to be recovered from foreign entities. At the same time, 73.9 percent of this figure, which is the one that can represent a net flow of income to the country, was in its term of recovery established, and only the 26.1 percent was out of term.

These analyses confirmed that there is sufficient cash payment management of accounts in freely convertible currency. The outstanding balances generally correspond to the country's normal income flows.

Finally, taking into consideration the cash payments, we have adopted measures that will improve management and ensure that these accumulations do not occur in the future. These measures are currently being implemented.

As for stimulating savings, approximately 59 percent of liquidity is deposited in savings accounts. Therefore, they are indispensable when analyzing measures to guarantee that that money stays in the banks.

There are some options that are not always linked to higher interest rates. Given the excess money supply in our country, raising interest rates would not necessarily stimulate more savings. Other ways have to be explored.

These include linking savings accounts to specific uses, and some of them in the workers' parliaments themselves. These accounts entail an immobilization of funds for a given period of time, with a bank guarantee for the saver, so that they become some sort of special savings bond. We also will analyze the feasibility of setting savings accounts at fixed terms in foreign currency.

These measures should guarantee the immobilization of that majoritarian saving figure that we have deposited in the banks and that furthermore must increase, because it is convenient, for the country, an increment of the savings. It is convenient that the measures we adopt preserve the mechanisms that stimulate savings; though, on the other hand, we have to make sure that that amount of money stays out of circulation for as long as possible.

We also evaluated an idea that emerged from the workers' parliaments to issue public debt bonds. This is a measure that has not been used for years in our country. But they are a means for the state (and one wisely used in other countries) to request a domestic loan from its population, payable in the long term, generally ten, fifteen, or twenty years. We can test several variants of this type of debt issuance.

We must gradually have better control of the circulation of freely convertible currency in the country. This is a new phenomenon that we began to face last year. We still do not have enough experience with its implications and the measures that we will have to adopt. We are considering some of the ideas that came from the workers' parliaments such as exchanging foreign currency for a currency playing that role—it could be called a convertible peso or currency peso. It offers advantages, since this monetary circulation would be under the direct and sovereign authority of the Cuban state. It is one of the options we have to consider.

There are also measures that would strengthen the circulation of the peso by offsetting the imbalance created when freely convertible currency is introduced into circulation.

We also must consider ways to incentivize workers to increase the offer of products or services in national currency and in accordance with the needs of the country.

Some measures of this kind recently have been implemented with electric power workers. This could lead, when we have more production, to the deregulated sale of certain products, at prices reflecting the situation we face because of the financial imbalances in the country. This does not exclude the possibility of analyzing idle inventories, or certain reserves, that could be included on this distribution channel.

Services that could be offered include personal insurance policies and insurance policies associated with goods and civil liability that have not been utilized in the country. This is something we must consider and evaluate as a complementary mechanism that provides risk protection to the population without drawing on the state's budget.

There are other measures, for example, advance collection with some discounts, of debts with Banco Popular de Ahorro resulting from personal credit or related to housing payments.

We have analyzed how the application of reasonable interest discount rates linked to immediate or short-term payment could raise between 300 and 500 million pesos.

We also must analyze measures to evaluate prices and tariffs. Comrade Ross has presented different opinions from the workers' parliaments, and we are evaluating some of that, either because of their economic relevance or level of consensus.

For example, we have evaluated the elimination of subsidies to products and replacing them with subsidies to low-income persons. This is within our possibilities and it could yield, in the short term, around 200 million pesos a year.

As for the increase of prices of non-essential items, several possibilities have been mentioned but there is consensus [regarding some measures], including increasing the price of cigarettes.

Minister Rodriguez cited other possibilities, including graduated pricing for alcoholic drinks and motor fuel; higher rates for electric

SAVED THE CUBAN REVOLUTION   85

power, telephone, postal, and transportation services; and charging for sports and cultural activities and for food in workers' cafeterias and in schools. He noted that some suggestions regarding public health were unacceptable because they conflicted with principles of the Revolution, such as charging for ambulance services.

Minister Rodriguez spoke about one of the most controversial measures: the institution of an income tax system.

> In the workers' parliaments there was clear opposition to an income tax. Let's remember, however, that the income tax would not only be applicable to salary earners but also to freelance workers.

Taxing the earnings of the approximately 153,000 freelance workers, he said, could bring in 126 million pesos. Minister Rodriguez also raised the possibility of taxing foreign currency income (but not remittances from abroad), houses and land, transportation, and water.

THE DEBATE

The two interventions—our presentation of the proposals contributed by more than three million workers in the workers' parliaments and Minister José Luis Rodríguez's discussion of measures that the National assembly could submit for the government's consideration—provided ideas that were ready to be implemented. Some interventions showed that revolutionary passion still required to arm itself with deeper concrete knowledge. In this respect, Fidel emphasized that we were still very far from being fully aware of the difficulties our economy was facing.

When speaking with the deputies and reflecting on both the discussions in the previous Assembly session in December and the workers' parliaments, Fidel made it clear that our main priority was to preserve workers' salaries. He added that we also had revalue salaries and the peso.

He referred to the heroism of the workers who were harvesting sugarcane on May 1, a Sunday. He noted that although most Cubans were doing their part, others were not. He likened the latter to an illness that was affecting the body's overall health. Fidel pointed out that the excess money supply was a cancer and that its origin was the Special Period.

He added, "We must calculate properly the things we can do so that the problem is not repeated. To prevent this cancer from reproducing. To extirpate it from its roots definitively. We have discussed these problems with the people, with the masses, and we will discuss them here, in depth. We must discuss them with the highest degree of democracy in the world."

He emphasized that Cuba faced a world totally dominated by and under the hegemony of neoliberal capitalism. We would not surrender but rather had to adapt to those realities, under a blockade imposed by the world's greatest military and economic power. He observed that because the enemy was working overtime to discourage and demoralize our people, we had to raise their morale and encourage their fighting spirit.

"We have demonstrated what many thought impossible, that after the collapse of the Socialist Bloc and of the Soviet Union, almost four years later, here is Cuba, the country they called [a Russian] satellite, now a heroic star ninety miles from the United States."

THE INTERNATIONAL SOLIDARITY OF TRADE UNIONISTS

The collapse of the Soviet Union and the dismantling of the Socialist Bloc at the end of the 1980s and the early 1990s had a devastating impact on the international trade union movement, a consequence of the political and ideological crises of the left.

Although many trade unions proclaimed their independence from any political organization, the truth is that most of them, both at the national and international levels, had aligned with social democratic parties and formations of the West, and communist and labor parties of Eastern Europe.

The Cold War also affected the trade union movement, with clear demarcations among the International Confederation of Free Trade

Union Organizations (CIOSL, in Spanish), in which the American Federation of Labor and Congress of Industrial Organizations (AFL-CIO) played a leading role, along with Britain's Trade Union Congress (TUC), and Japan's Confederation of Labor (RENGO), and on the other side, the World Trade Union Federation (FSM), comprising Soviet trade unions, France's General Confederation of Workers (CGT), and Cuba's CTC.

With the dismantling of the USSR and the socialist countries, many trade union organizations lost their referents. The crisis affected not only the former Socialist Bloc but also militant southern European labor organizations: Spain's Workers' Commissions (CCOO), Italy's Italian General Confederation of Labor (CGIL), and France's CGT. Asian, African, and Latin American organizations that had maintained close links with communist and revolutionary parties also experienced this disorientation.

The United States declared that it won the Cold War, with the supposed triumph of U.S.-style bourgeois democracy proclaimed as "the end of history."[21] The so-called Washington Consensus entailed brutal neoliberal policies, including the dismantling of historic labor and social achievements and the weakening of trade unions.[22] Ronald Reagan in the United States and Margaret Thatcher in the United Kingdom inflicted severe blows on unionized workers, including the deregulation of labor markets through financial adjustments and the dominance of transnational capital.

For many years, the CTC and Cuban unions were attacked by the CIOSL and mainly by its U.S. subsidiary, the Inter-American Regional Workers Organization (ORIT), which, under the dominance of AFL-CIO, dictated the CIOSL's anti-communist and pro-imperialist political line.

The International Labor Organization (ILO) was, for many years, the main mechanism by which CIOSL and ORIT orchestrated their campaigns against Cuba and its trade union movement, following the imperial policies dictated from Washington. Despite that, the Cuban Revolution's international prestige among workers generated sympathy and solidarity with millions of workers, many of whom confronted the leadership of their unions to demand reestablished relations with the Cuban people and its workers.

There was no congress or trade union conference anywhere where workers and trade unions did not demand the presence of CTC and its unions, even though they had to defray the costs of our participation. An impressive solidarity and support movement was being forged, in opposition to the interference in Cuba by the United States and the international finance institutions.

During those years, May Day celebrations brought hundreds of thousands of trade union activists and leaders to Cuba, from all over the globe. They would fill our squares to demonstrate their solidarity with Cuba and their condemnation of the U.S. blockade.

In 1997, when Cuba was undergoing a profound economic crisis, with shortages of all kinds, CTC called an international meeting against the Free Trade Area of the Americas (FTAA) and neoliberal globalization.[23] The presence in Havana of more than 1,200 trade unionists representing more than 300 trade union organizations constituted an event of historic significance. The meeting marked the first instance of a global protest by workers and their unions against the scourge of neoliberalism.

From that moment on, the CTC and Cuban trade unions would annually receive delegations from the main trade union organizations of many countries, strengthening the links of collaboration and solidarity. It is not possible to list all of them, but I must particularly acknowledge the Cuba Solidarity Campaign organized by TUC and the British trade unions. The public services union UNISON also played an outstanding role, sending three ships carrying ambulances, buses, surgical material, medications, public health uniforms, and other important items.

There were as well significant contributions from France's CGT, Spain's General Union of Workers (UGT) and CCOO, Italy's CGIL, the Canadian Labor Conference (CLC), and from trade union organizations in Greece, Denmark, Norway, Germany, and Portugal. There even were efforts within CIOSL to undermine the isolation of and hostility toward the CTC.

SAVED THE CUBAN REVOLUTION

How could we forget the moral and material support from French graphic workers, who, under the leadership of their trade union in Paris, organized a contingent of ships that brought us donations of many products we lacked, including ink, paper, and printing equipment for our main national newspapers.

We remember with great affection the selfless and militant solidarity of the Congress of South African Trade Unions (COSATU), as well as the solidarity expressed by China, Vietnam, and India.

The close relations built with major Latin American and Caribbean trade union organizations were propitious for mutual solidarity and coordination of common action against neoliberalism and imperialism, including opposition to the FTAA. These organizations included CUT (Central Única dos Trabalhadores, United Workers Central) and other Brazilian trade union organizations, Uruguay's Intersyndical Plenary of Workers-National Workers' Convention (PIT-CNT), the Argentinian trade unions, Peru's Workers' General Confederation (CGT), Panama's Workers' National Trade Union (CNTP), Mexico's Trade Union of Electricians (SME), and the trade union organizations of Jamaica and the Dominican Republic.

I also must acknowledge the selfless and deeply humane support from the Pastors for Peace Movement, led by Lucius Walker,[24] and of the Cuba Friendship Associations of various countries.

The militant solidarity of trade unions, their workers, and other organizations helped us to confront the U.S. blockade, and to overcome the impact of international crises without sacrificing our principles and aspirations.

CONCLUSIONS

After the triumph of the Revolution, Cuba faced constant shortages of resources, food, medications, fuel, raw materials and materials of all kinds, for transportation, and fertilizers for our farms. Cubans felt the impact of these shortages in their workplaces and in their quality of life. Cubans endured, for example, many hours without electricity.

We cannot speak about those Special Period years without

highlighting the role of Cuban women, who, as workers, mothers, and housewives, carried a huge burden. Their inventiveness and perseverance was essential not only to dealing with the rigors of everyday life but also to making progress under such unfavorable conditions.

The great majority of Cubans decided that their only option was to resist, trusting that no one would be abandoned to their fate and that the country would do everything necessary to move forward. It was truly a colossal effort. Many difficulties were overcome; essential achievements of the Revolution and socialism were preserved under very complex conditions. There were many lessons learned about being prepared for adverse circumstances.

Our experiences during the Special Period, the organization and development of the workers' parliaments, and the widespread consensus we achieved will be studied by future generations. Cuba survived the crises caused by the dissolution of the Soviet Union and the Socialist Bloc. Those events led to the loss of stable economic relations that for almost thirty years were the basis of our development programs. At the same time, Cuba was contending with the reinforcement of the U.S. blockade imposed in the Revolution's early years. The foresight of Cuba's leaders, and particularly Fidel Castro's tenacity and perseverance, was critical to educating our people about the crises and strengthening their spirit of resistance and will to overcome. Cuba's press, intellectuals, and cultural workers also played critical roles in helping the country navigate the turbulent waters of the Special Period.

IN PART TWO OF THIS BOOK, I examine the historical antecedents of the events described in Part One. Resistance and resiliency have characterized the Cuban people since the founding of the nation. This history is indispensable to understanding Cubans' collective heroism under the extraordinarily adverse factors of the Special Period.

PART TWO

To understand how Cubans responded to the crises of the Special Period requires familiarity with milestones of our history of rebellion and resistance. It begins with the indigenous peoples who resisted the European colonizers, continues in the independence struggles against Spanish colonialism, then through three U.S. military occupations,[25] the years of the neocolonial Republic, and the economic and social conditions that led to the assault on the Moncada fortress July 26, 1953, organized and led by Fidel Castro. There followed the guerrilla and underground clandestine struggles from 1956 to 1958, and, with the triumph of the Revolution in 1959, the construction of a new society.

THE NIGHTMARE OF A DEVASTATING HURRICANE

To begin, we must look back to the immense cruelty that characterized the discovery, conquest, and colonization of Cuba by Europeans. The indigenous peoples were subjected to the most horrendous barbarism, which, in the words of our own Don Fernando Ortiz, was like the nightmare of a devastating hurricane—two worlds that discovered and collided with one another, and whose impact was terrible.[26]

Of course, the indigenes did not meekly resign themselves to the conquistadors' cruel domination. On the contrary, they tenaciously resisted. Among the most celebrated fighters was the sixteenth-century Taino *cacique* (chief) Hatuey, who after leading a rebellion in Hispaniola, emigrated to Cuba. He was considered the first chief that fought for the freedom of the island, in a precarious but astute and tenacious guerrilla war against the colonizers. He was hunted, surprised, and captured, then sentenced to burn at the stake. But others, emerging from their refuges, attacked the invaders. Another Taino *cacique*, Guamá, led uprisings in the early 1500s against the Spanish *encomenderos* (masters) who exploited and killed the indigenous people.[27]

Africans, uprooted from their lands to be enslaved in the Americas, also did not resign themselves to their condition. Cuban historical accounts include frequent references to *palenques* (hiding places) of Black *cimarrones* (fugitives), riots, and uprisings. In March 1812, a free

94 HOW THE WORKERS' PARLIAMENTS

Black man, José Antonio Aponte, led an uprising in eastern Havana that was quickly suppressed by the colonial forces.[28] In November 1843, a Black woman named Carlota led a revolt at the Triunvirato sugar plantation in Matanzas. She was savagely murdered, her body tied to horses pulling in opposing directions until she was dismembered. In the 1844 revolt known as the "Stairway Conspiracy"[29] many enslaved people, free Black, and mixed-race men lost their lives, among them, the poet Gabriel de la Concepción Valdés.[30]

THE ORIGINS OF CUBAN NATIONALITY

In Cuba, the mix of the original indigenous population, Europeans, and Africans not only produced a new culture but also uprooted a preceding culture. A new social subject emerged, the Creole, who was not a colonial settler but native to the island.

The manifestations of an emerging Cuban nationality, expressed in literature and other cultural production during the last three decades of the eighteenth century, would be followed by political tendencies that proposed various solutions to the island's colonial status. The different schools of thought comprised reformism, autonomy, and even annexation to the United States. There also were Cubans with pro-independence ideas, radicals influenced by the late eighteenth- and early nineteenth-century emancipation struggles in the Americas: the Declaration of Independence of the thirteen English colonies in North America, the Haitian Revolution, and the independence movements in Latin America between 1820 and 1830.

The reformers were dealt a devastating blow in 1867 when Spain failed to revise its colonial policy in Cuba. Madrid gave no consideration to Cuban aspirations for economic, political, and social reform. It became evident that the only real option was to organize an independence movement. Soon one emerged, mostly in eastern Cuba, and with significant strength in Bayamo, Manzanillo, and Camagüey.

The movement initiated in the east extended to other neighboring jurisdictions. In August and September 1867, the Revolutionary Committee of Bayamo convened a meeting of independence forces.

They decided to launch an uprising at the end of the sugarcane harvest. Carlos Manuel de Céspedes, a Cuban-born planter from Manzanillo, along with other important figures, set October 14, 1868, as the day of the uprising. But after the Spanish discovered the plan, the date was changed to October 10.

That day, Cespedes issued a manifesto for Cuban independence from his sugar plantation, La Demajagua. The manifesto called for an all-out military uprising against the Spanish. It also called for slavery to be abolished, albeit gradually and with indemnification of slave owners. After the uprising, the rebel forces stormed Bayamo. On November 4, patriots from Camagüey rose up, in Las Clavellinas. On February 6, 1869, the uprising spread to Villa Clara, but there the independence fighters faced a resource shortage and heavy resistance from the Spanish forces, which were determined to prevent the uprising from reaching the rich sugar zones of western Cuba, the center of Spanish power and of the slaveholding bourgeoisie. The Spanish military command organized a rapid advance on Bayamo, the capital of the insurrection, which fell in January 1869. Rather than surrender, insurrectionary forces and the local population burned the city.

Thus began a ten-year war for independence. Cuban troops fought with great tenacity and bravery, enduring privations imposed by the difficult conditions of the jungles. The independence fighters, comprising Cubans of different social classes, including enslaved and free Blacks and mixed-race people, raised their *mambí* (machetes) against the colonialist forces. The Spanish called them *mambíses* because of their use of this weapon; the term was meant to be derogatory, but the rebels accepted it and used it with pride.

In numerous military actions, such important figures as Máximo Gómez,[31] Ignacio Agramonte,[32] and others emerged. Particularly notable was Antonio Maceo Grajales, who took up arms on October 12, 1868, two days after the conflict began. Maceo, the son of a mixed-race Venezuelan father and a Black Cuban mother, was a master military tactician and a prestigious officer who attained the rank of major general.

The Cuban Liberation Army, however, suffered from disunity and internal contradictions, notwithstanding its brilliant military

96 HOW THE WORKERS' PARLIAMENTS

operations and the courage and self-sacrifice of its troops. There were numerous efforts to achieve unity, including the meeting at Guáimaro in April 1869, which produced the first constitution of the Republic in Arms. This event fostered a democratic tradition in the revolutionary forces and demonstrated the leadership's commitment to the common cause of independence.

Nevertheless, there remained significant differences over how the independence struggle should be waged. Of special significance, on October 27, 1873, a Cuban tribunal dismissed Céspedes, who had been elected president of the Republic in Arms in Guáimaro. He subsequently moved to San Lorenzo, in Sierra Maestra, where on February 27, 1874, he was discovered and shot by Spanish soldiers.

As 1877 was coming to a close, the crisis—both military and civil— in the revolutionary forces was profound. The exhaustion of the patriotic forces after more than nine years of war, in the midst of scarce resources, a lack of external support, and deepening internal contradictions in the revolutionary ranks, resulted, on February 10, 1878, in the Pact of Zanjón, which ended the war.

When Antonio Maceo learned about the pact, he regrouped his troops and wrote to the main officers to raise their morale. On March 14, he met with several *mambí* chiefs who answered his call. He knew that the colonial government's peace proposal was an acknowledgment that it could never militarily defeat the *mambíses*. The next day, in Mangos de Baraguá, he led one of the most significant events in the independence struggle: the Protest of Baraguá, where he rejected a peace treaty that did not grant independence or abolish slavery. On March 23, hostilities resumed. However, the situation of the Cuban rebels was becoming unsustainable. The provisional government established in Baraguá granted Antonio Maceo safe conduct from Cuba; on May 9, 1878, he set off for Jamaica. His plan was to obtain resources to return and continue the war, but that was not possible. The revolution begun on October 10, 1868, had come to an end.

The Ten-Year War did not bring independence, but it served to forge and consolidate the Cuban nationality. Referring to that milestone of our history, Cintio Vitier[33] said, "It taught the Cuban, above

SAVED THE CUBAN REVOLUTION

all the deceptions, the true face of the Homeland and, in the clamor of combat, the Homeland became visible to all."[34]

A FECUND TRUCE

The end of the Ten-Year War (also known as *Guerra Grande,* the Big War) did not lessen the yearning for independence. Indeed, Cuban patriots, in exile and in Cuba, were preparing a new armed uprising. At the end of 1878, expatriates elected General Calixto García president of the Cuban Revolutionary Committee.[35]

In 1879, uprisings occurred in eastern and central Cuba. But the arms and other resources that were expected to arrive never came. Maceo could not disembark on Cuban coasts as he had hoped. After several attempts, Calixto García managed to touch land in May 1880. However, ill and unable to contact troops in the East and cut off from those in Las Villas, he accepted a pardon and surrendered.

In this *Guerra Chiquita* (Little War) in 1879, the second of three conflicts between Cuban rebels and Spain, the independence forces were poorly organized and lacked political coherence. However, the Little War turned out to be valuable in preparing for a new conflict, in which unity in the independence struggle would be achieved by José Martí.

MARTÍ'S LEGACY

In the late nineteenth century, Cuba demanded profound economic and social change. José Martí played a crucial role in this phase of Cuban history. A poet born in Havana to Spanish parents, Martí was a political prisoner and an exile before he was eighteen years old. In fact, he spent much of his life in exile from Cuba. From Spain, he denounced the horrors of colonialism. In Mexico, Guatemala, and Venezuela, he came in contact with Latin American cultural spheres and learned the history and contemporary reality of the region's indigenous peoples. He assumed as his own the hopes and wishes of exploited Black, mixed-race, indigenous, and white Cubans. In 1881, he would write: "Of America I'm its son: my duty is to it."[36]

98 HOW THE WORKERS' PARLIAMENTS

He was a teacher, a diplomat, and an organizer. As a journalist, he promoted progressive ideas and causes. A brilliant orator and person of extraordinary culture, he fought indefatigably for Cuba's freedom.

Martí's ultimate purpose was to unite the generation of the ten-year Big War. with the young revolutionaries whom he called *pinos nuevos* (new pines). He contacted Big War veterans, proposed ideas and arguments, and devoted all his energies to rebuilding confidence in the independence movement among old and new combatants, and among Cubans from every social class. His work resulted in the creation of the Cuban Revolutionary Party,[37] whose aim was Cuban independence but which also encouraged Puerto Rican independence advocates. Martí sought to prevent U.S. expansion into the Southern Hemisphere. With exceptional foresight, he warned about the dangers the emergent U.S. empire posed not only for Cuba but for the world.

Martí sowed hopes and inspired profound feelings of humanism and solidarity. His thought and action made him a figure who transcended his time and national borders to become the most universal of all Cubans. He is an exemplar of Latin-Americanism, anti-racism, and anti-imperialism.

With extraordinary intelligence and sensitivity, he organized the final phase of Cuba's struggle for independence from Spain. He prepared what he called the *Guerra Necesaria* (Necessary War). In December 1894, Martí directed and organized, from exile in New York City, the Fernandina Plan, which was to bring three military expeditions to Cuba. However, the Necessarian plan was betrayed, and the United States prevented the vessels from setting sail. Nevertheless, revolutionaries in Cuba were authorized to initiate an insurrection, on February 24, 1895, without the expeditionary forces.

Uprisings were to occur simultaneously in different parts of the country, but they instead broke out in eastern Cuba, led by multiple pro-independence forces. On March 25, 1895, José Martí and Máximo Gómez, in their respective capacities as Delegate of the Cuban Revolutionary Party and General in Chief, signed the Manifesto of Montecristi, which constituted the programmatic basis of the revolution.[38]

SAVED THE CUBAN REVOLUTION 99

The miscarried Fernandina Plan and Martí's call to begin the war without the expeditionary forces meant that by February 24, 1895, when the campaign began, none of the main military chiefs was in Cuba. Yet, in the midst of very unfavorable conditions, the armed independence struggle was resumed.

Antonio Maceo and Flor Crombet,[39] as chief of the expedition, arrived on April 1 in Duaba, near Baracoa, on Cuba's north coast. On April 11, in Playitas de Cajobabo, at the southeastern edge of the island, José Martí and Máximo Gómez, along with other patriots, touched Cuban soil. On May 5, at the La Mejorana plantation in eastern Cuba, Martí, Gómez, and Maceo met. There are no records of their discussions, no meeting minutes or official statements from its participants. However, Martí's notes indicate that it was a tense meeting.[40] Historian Rolando Rodríguez described the meeting and its three participants:

> After all, it was now almost the case that they had chosen the endeavor, but that the endeavor had chosen them, because in light of its colossal, Cyclops-like nature, it required lions, and lions do not stroke each other. The three of them, the refined, seductive, and brilliant Martí; the vigorous, energetic, and talented Maceo; the abrupt, astute, and hardworking Gómez, were men made to give orders and lead, each in his own way, and not to be ordered. Their relationships could not be, therefore, easy, and that explains their differences. If they had been some other way, possibly their names would have never entered history or if so, it would have been as subordinates.[41]

At noon on May 19, 1895, in Dos Ríos, José Martí died the way he wanted to—"facing the sun."[42] This was a hard blow for the newly reborn revolution. Martí's eminence in the anticolonial struggle came from his organizational abilities and the soundness of his ideas and ideological conceptions. No other figure, during the 1895 Revolution or in the first five decades of the coming century, would offer the same combination of unremitting and unconditional dedication and intellectual leadership.

On October 22, 1895, Antonio Maceo initiated his advance toward

100   HOW THE WORKERS' PARLIAMENTS

the West from Baraguá, the site of the historic 1878 protests. While in
Villa Clara, he met with Máximo Gómez, who designated him Chief of
the Invading Column.

At the beginning of 1896, the Mambese Army had already reached
the capital. Maceo continued to Pinar del Río, while Gómez remained
in Havana. Maceo, pursued by Spanish troops, led several campaigns
until his January 22 arrival in Mantua, the westernmost point in Pinar
del Río.

Cuban victory was just a matter of resistance and time. Spain, however, refused to relinquish its colony. General Valeriano Weyler was
appointed to lead the colonialist troops. His re-concentration policy,
imposed first in Pinar del Río and then in other regions, sought to
deter peasants from supporting the Mambese rebels by forcibly relocating them to towns and cities. The peasants' homes were burned and
their possessions destroyed. Subjected to hunger and exposed to epidemics, they suffered enormous losses. It was genocide. However, the
war did not stop. The ranks of the Liberation Army kept increasing, as
did the resistance of the Cuban people.

Antonio Maceo, heeding the call of Máximo Gómez from Las Villas,
entered Havana from the sea on December 4, 1896. Three days later, in
San Pedro, near the capital, the leader popularly known as the Bronze
Titan was killed in combat. His assistant, Francisco Gómez Toro, the
son of Máximo Gómez, also lost his life.

After Maceo's death, Calixto García, Chief of the Eastern Department,
became the Deputy General of the Liberation Army. Máximo Gómez
was establishing his La Reforma campaign in the island's center. The
enemy was being battered, militarily and by the Caribbean climate and
the spread of disease among its troops. The victory of the Cuban forces
was imminent.

THE IMPERIALIST INTERVENTION OF
THE UNITED STATES

Long before the beginning of the armed fight for Cuban independence,
successive U.S. governments tried to economically and politically

SAVED THE CUBAN REVOLUTION 101

control Cuba through various means—attempting to purchase or annex its territory and to oppose its independence. On February 15, 1898, an explosion sank the USS *Maine*, a battleship, in Havana harbor. The United States had sent the Navy vessel to Havana on the pretext of protecting U.S. citizens in the island during Cuba's war for independence from Spain. The cause of the explosion remains disputed. But it served its purpose: to provide a fig leaf for the United States to directly intervene in Cuba's long war for independence.

When these events took place, the Liberation Army dominated most of the Cuban countryside, using guerilla tactics to attack Spanish forces. Spain suffered constant losses, not only in battle with insurrectionary fighters, but also because of epidemics of cholera, yellow fever, and malaria. Additionally, Cuba's tropical climate proved insalubrious for the Spanish troops.

In April 1898, the U.S. Congress approved a so-called joint resolution, which established that "the Island of Cuba is, and by right must be, free and independent." Despite its language, the resolution opened the way for U.S. intervention. Spain and the United States broke off diplomatic relations. The United States blockaded and bombed several Cuban ports as a prelude to its military invasion. The Spanish-American War was now underway.

The U.S. forces disembarked in Oriente province, which the Liberation Army controlled. U.S. commanding officers and General Calixto García Íñiguez, who led the Cuban troops, agreed on a plan for the U.S. forces to enter the southern part of the province. The Cuban troops undertook actions to clear the coast, and U.S. forces landed June 22 and 23, 1898.

On July 3, the Spanish squadron was destroyed in a naval battle in Santiago de Cuba Bay. The mambeses surrounded the city to impede the arrival of the Spaniards. On July 17, the Spanish forces surrendered. The Cuban troops, however, were blocked from entering Santiago de Cuba. Calixto Garcia responded to this affront in a letter to the chief of the U.S. troops: "We are not a savage people who do not know the principles of the civilized war; we form a poor and ragged army, as poor and ragged as was the army of your ancestors in your noble war for the independence of the United States; but, like the heroes of Saratoga and Yorktown, we respect our cause too much as to tarnish it with barbarity and cowardice." [43]

In August, the United States and Spain signed an armistice. The Cuban forces had no part in the negotiations between the two imperial powers. On December 10, 1898, Spain and the United States signed the Treaty of Paris, once again without Cuban representation. The treaty granted the United States temporary control of Cuba and ceded ownership of Puerto Rico, Guam, and the Philippine Islands. The United States paid Spain $20 million for the Philippines. José Martí's warnings about U.S. imperialist expansion now proved prescient.

The United States moved to dissolve the representative bodies of the Cuban people and to disarm and dissolve the Liberation Army. Tomás Estrada Palma, who had been President of the Cuban Republic in Arms during the Ten-Year War, became the Delegate of the Cuban Revolutionary Party after José Martí's death. He instituted changes to the party that deviated from Martí's conception and structure, finally dissolving it on December 21, 1898, claiming that it had no reason to exist. On December 31, the final edition of *Patria*, the newspaper that Martí founded and which had contributed so much to the independence struggle, was published.

On January 1, 1899, Spain officially relinquished its legal powers over Cuba to the U.S. Armed Forces. The first U.S. military governor established seven administrative areas and appointed generals to head each one. While retaining supreme authority, he appointed civil governors in the provinces and mayors and council members in the municipalities. Many former functionaries of the Spanish colonial government retained their positions. The United States created the Rural Guard to protect the interests of the big landowners and the sugarcane bourgeoisie as well as a police corps at the service of the occupation government.

The Spanish-American War, launched by the United States on the pretext of liberating Cuba from Spain, was a conflict that exchanged territories between two imperial powers, one a declining empire, the other a rising one. The long, heroic Cuban fight for its independence resulted in the hegemony of a new colonial power, the United States.

There was opposition to the U.S. occupation by officers of the Liberation Army, revolutionary émigrés, middle-class radicals, and the Cuban labor movement. There was sharp criticism of the Treaty of Paris, which had been negotiated without any Cuban involvement. The treaty excluded Isla de Pinos (Isle of Pines) from Cuban territory. The treaty did not set a deadline for the end of the U.S. occupation. Cuba was now subservient to the United States and to U.S. capital.

Although some Cubans supported annexation to the United States, opposition and resistance grew, in defense of Cuba's sovereignty. Some in the United States were sympathetic to Cuba's independence struggle, while others feared that annexation might harm American economic interests by ending the tax-free entry of Cuban products to the United States. These factors led the U.S. government to consider making its military occupation provisional and to permit establishment of a constituent assembly, the holding of general elections, and the eventual transfer of power to Cubans.

A constituent convention was convened to draw up and adopt a constitution, which was approved February 21, 1901. Because former mambíses participated in the convention, the new constitution acknowledged to some degree Cuban aspirations. These acknowledgments, however, were limited, reflecting the heterogeneity of the convention's participants and their positions. Some delegates were pro-independence, others were moderate nationalists, and others pro-annexation.

THE PLATT AMENDMENT

In February 1901, the U.S. Congress approved the Platt Amendment, which established conditions for the withdrawal of U.S. forces while actually solidifying U.S. dominance over Cuba. The Platt Amendment established that all acts by the United States during its military occupation of Cuba were valid. It included the Treaty of Paris provision that removed the Isla de Pinos from Cuban territory.

The amendment also stipulated that the government of Cuba would sell or lease to the United States lands deemed necessary for the establishment of coal mines and naval stations.

So much for Cuban sovereignty.

Although some supported what was essentially an annexation, there was a wave of protests in several parts of Cuba. The United States gave an ultimatum: Cuba must accept the entire Platt Amendment as an appendix to the Cuban Constitution or the occupation troops would not withdraw.

Although the Cuban assembly initially rejected the Amendment, it was accepted on June 12 by a vote of sixteen to eleven, with four abstentions. It was then integrated into the 1901 Cuban Constitution. Elections were called for December 31, 1901, with two candidates for President of the Republic: Tomás Estrada Palma and General Bartolomé Masó. The former favored the U.S. interests; the latter opposed all U.S. intervention and the Platt Amendment. The occupation regime put all its power behind Estrada Palma's candidacy.

Given the strong likelihood of electoral fraud and obvious political chicanery, Bartolomé Masó withdrew his candidacy. Running unopposed, Estrada Palma, who held U.S. citizenship and resided in the United States, became the first president of the new republic. He took office May 20, 1902, the date that marked the end of the first U.S. military intervention in Cuba.

The Estrada Palma government (1902–1906) represented the fulfillment of the Platt Amendment. On May 22, 1903, Cuba entered into a treaty with the United States that allowed the United States to intervene unilaterally in Cuban affairs. The treaty also included a pledge to lease land to the United States for its naval bases on the island. The treaty additionally gave the United States control over Cuban markets and set preferential customs rates for U.S. products with minimal benefits for Cuban exports. This accentuated the unequal exchange between the two nations, resulting in the stagnation of Cuban agriculture and industry. The Platt Amendment violated Cuban sovereignty, and the Treaty of Commercial Reciprocity (a misnomer, given its inequitable nature) wrecked its economy.

On July 2, 1903, an agreement was signed that leased Bahía Honda, on Cuba's north shore, to the United States for a naval base, for $2,000

SAVED THE CUBAN REVOLUTION   105

in gold per year. (In 1912, the United States abandoned it for an expansion of its naval base in Guantánamo Bay, which it still occupies.) The United States committed itself to satisfying Cuban claims over the Isla de Pinos, but the U.S. Senate refused to allow it.

The first years of the Republic were characterized by increased penetration of foreign capital and the failure to fund reconstruction of areas ravaged by war. Both circumstances generated discontent among the population and led to protests.

Estrada Palma intended to run for reelection in 1905. Once again, electoral fraud occurred, leading to the withdrawal from the process of the Liberal Party, whose candidate was General José Miguel Gómez (1858–1921). And once again, Estrada Palma was the sole candidate, but in August 1906, insurrections broke out in parts of the country. Despite the mediation of veterans of the independence struggle, Estrada Palma demanded total surrender and moved against liberal leaders, bringing an increase of imprisonment and crime. The so-called August Little War was intensified. Estrada Palma did not try to achieve agreement among Cubans; instead, he requested a new U.S. military intervention.

THE SECOND OCCUPATION OF CUBA BY THE UNITED STATES

Under the second U.S. occupation (1906–1909), the Cuban Congress was suspended; the militias created by Estrada Palma were dissolved; and U.S. supervisors were appointed for the Rural Guard. Misuse of public funds was common, and political and administrative corruption were pervasive. The Cuban Republic suffered from indebtedness and bribery. The "bottle" (no-show jobs) became a common practice. Public works projects were fruitful sources of embezzlement. Workers and their demands were repressed, and armed uprisings against the occupation were crushed.

The second U.S. occupation of Cuba ended in 1908, with the electoral victory of a liberal candidate, José Miguel Gómez.

FIRST GOVERNMENTS OF THE NEO-COLONIAL REPUBLIC

From the end of the second U.S. occupation in 1909 to 1933, Cuba had several presidents, all pro-independence, whose administrations nonetheless flouted Martí's aspirations for a democratic and truly sovereign republic. The country was in debt, its economy subordinated to the interests of U.S. capital. The aspirations of the great majority of Cubans were sidelined. Frustration mounted, but the Cuban people demonstrated their will to resist. Protests and strikes occurred, which were met with harsh repression. When in 1913 members of the Partido Independiente de Color (Independence Party of Color/PIC) led a revolt in Oriente, they were suppressed with extreme brutality. Thousands of Blacks were killed, while the armed forces suffered only ten losses.[44]

The First World War (1914–1918) spurred a rapid expansion of sugar production to compensate for the loss of the beetroot harvest in Europe. Sugar prices rose, and for a while generated wealth for Cuba. This development also consolidated the monocrop basis of the Cuban economy. The prosperity it generated benefited the sugar producers and monopolies, commercial interests, and banks. The Cuban masses experienced product shortages and steep increases in the cost of living.

When the First World War ended, European sugar production recovered. With so much sugar in international markets, prices fell. From May to December 1920, the price of a pound of sugar on the world market fell from 22.5 cents to 3.75 cents.

But in the postwar years, signs of resistance began to appear. Workers became more organized, and more Cubans demanded the annulment or modification of the onerous Treaty of Commercial Reciprocity.

On March 18, 1923, thirteen young male intellectuals issued a written protest against the government's purchase of the Santa Clara Convent at an exorbitant price while the country was undergoing an economic crisis. The attorney and poet Rubén Martínez Villena was a leader of the "Protest of the Thirteen," which led to the resignation of the Secretary of Justice, whom the protesters had accused of fraud.[45]

During the trial of the thirteen protesters, a small number of journalists, attorneys, and artists formed the Grupo Minorista (Minority Group), an informal association that advocated leftist political and cultural policies. They represented the emergence of a new generation of socially and politically engaged intellectuals at a time, the mid-1920s, when Cuba was experiencing profound political and social shockwaves, including repercussions of capitalism's global crises.

THE MACHADO DICTATORSHIP

The stagnation of the sugar industry and of the entire Cuban economy was becoming more pronounced. Social and political conflict increased as did protests against U.S. interference in Cuba. Cuba's ruling class sought reforms that would preserve the system and weaken the revolutionary movement. The best option was Gerardo Machado y Morales, the Liberal Party candidate for president in 1924.[46] Machado, who was closely linked to specific sectors of U.S. capital in Cuba, led one of the bloodiest tyrannies of the neocolonial republic.

Julio Antonio Mella was one of Machado's most prominent victims. A student of law and philosophy, Mella founded the Federation of University Students. He also organized the First National Congress of Students and founded the José Martí Popular University to provide political and academic instruction to workers. He founded the Anticlerical League and the Cuban section of the Anti-Imperialist League of the Americas. He was expelled from the university for his revolutionary activities. In November 1925, Mella was arrested and jailed. While in prison, he went on a hunger strike. The Mella Pro-Freedom Committee initiated a campaign on his behalf, and national and international pressures led to his release. Forced to leave Cuba, he moved to Mexico, where he connected with Latin American and other international revolutionary movements. He was assassinated January 10, 1929, in Mexico under orders of the dictator Machado.

There were several other important developments during the Machado years. On August 2, 1925, the *Confederación Nacional Obrera de Cuba* (National Working-Class Confederation of Cuba/ CNOC) was founded, during the Third National Working-Class

108 HOW THE WORKERS' PARLIAMENTS

Congress in Camagüey. Trade union leader Alfredo López Arencibia was instrumental in CNOC's adoption of pro-working-class policies.[47] On August 16, Carlos Baliño and Julio Antonio Mella founded the Communist Party of Cuba to link the independence struggle and the fight for social revolution.[48]

On April 7, 1927, young militants founded the University Student Directory. A few days later, its members were arrested. Once released, they went underground, and the organization was silenced.[49]

Machado intended to impose a prorogation of powers through a constitutional reform that would allow him to remain president for six years. Although this provoked opposition, even among bourgeois parties, Machado assumed a second six-year term in 1929, plunging the country into a political crisis.

In 1930, the disastrous effects of the world economic crisis hit Cuba hard. Conditions deteriorated, and repression grew. The neocolonial republic was exhausted. Opposition spread to many different groups and sectors of Cuban society. There were ideological and political divisions among them, but Machado's regime was weakening.

President Franklin Delano Roosevelt was considering a new approach to Latin America, which he called the Good Neighbor Policy.[50] This policy change abrogated the Platt Amendment. Roosevelt appointed Benjamin Sumner Welles, his new ambassador, to mediate between the Machado regime and its opponents. Welles went to Cuba in 1933 to assume this mission, but his mediation attempts failed.

The attorney Rubén Martínez Villena, although terminally ill with tuberculosis, organized and led a general revolutionary strike that was the *coup de grâce* to Machado and his tyrannical regime. But on August 7, 1933, Machado's forces machine-gunned a crowd that had gathered at the National Capitol, killing twenty and injuring one hundred. On August 12, Machado fled to the Bahamas. When Cubans heard that he was gone, they took to the streets all over the country. On August 12, 1933, Machado's former foreign minister, Carlos Manuel de Céspedes y Quesada, assumed the presidency.[51]

A popular uprising had overthrown the dictator, but the revolutionary forces could not assume power. Machado was gone, yet his government managed to survive. Unemployment and hunger spurred more opposition, including a general strike. As the Cuban opposition became more combative, U.S. warships in the Havana port readied their guns and marines prepared to disembark. In the Cuban army, insubordination became common, with soldiers ignoring their officers' commands and plotting against them.

THE SEPTEMBER 4 COUP D'ÉTAT AND THE 100 DAYS GOVERNMENT

On September 4, 1933, a military coup d'état overthrew the provisional government of Carlos Manuel de Céspedes y Quesada. The leaders of the *Revuelta de los sargentos* (Sergeants' Revolt) were joined by the University Student Directorate and other civil society organizations. On September 5, the insurgents took control of Havana and the country's interior. The coup met no resistance from either civil or military authorities.

The junta of officers and students formed a five-person administration known as the Executive Commission, or Pentarchy.[52] Pentarchy member Sergio Carbó, a journalist, drafted a proclamation signed by eighteen civilians and one sergeant: Fulgencio Batista. The proclamation was published in every Cuban newspaper. The insurgents stated their intentions to: rebuild the country's economy; establish a constituent assembly; achieve a rapid return to normality; and to punish those responsible for the Machado regime's repression. They pledged to protect the lives and properties of Cubans and foreigners and to assume the Republic's debts and commitments.

Sergio Carbó promoted Batista from sergeant to colonel without notifying the other four members. Both were ousted by the University Student Directorate and another Pentarchy member, Ramón Grau San Martín, a professor at the University of Havana School of Medicine, was named president. The Pentarchy had lasted only five days. On September 10, 1933, a new government was formed, with Grau its president. His government was heterogenous, comprising nationalist reformers (the majority tendency), pro-imperialist reactionaries

110 HOW THE WORKERS' PARLIAMENTS

(Batista and his supporters), and revolutionary leftists (led by the U.S.-born socialist Antonio Guiteras Holmes.[53]) Despite the profound differences among its leaders, the government adopted measures that benefited the Cuban masses. They included a minimum wage, labor regulations, academic freedom, and nationalization of important sectors of the economy.

But the country's situation was turbulent. Former officers of the Machado dictatorship and right-wing forces opposed the government; Grau generally supported Guiteras's positions but tolerated Batista's actions, including the colonel's violent repression of a general strike. Guiteras, Minister of the Interior, found himself caught between those who held him responsible for the massacres and right-wing forces.

Grau's 100 Days Government lasted until January 15, 1934, when Batista—who had been conspiring with U.S. diplomat Sumner Welles—forced him to resign. Grau was replaced by Carlos Mendieta, and within five days the United States recognized Cuba's new government. Students denounced the counterrevolution financed by foreign capital and backed by the United States. Between January 15 and 18, 1934, three presidents assumed power. Batista remained the leader of the Cuban army and was the government's actual head. The radical achievements of the 100 Days Government were rolled back, and Cuba entered a period of reactionary militarism.

On February 8, 1934, Eduardo Chibás[54] and Carlos Prío Socarrás[55] founded the Cuban Revolutionary Party, also known as the Authentic Party. The party was diverse but nationalist reformists dominated. In May 1934, Guiteras founded *Joven Cuba* (Young Cuba), a political organization inspired by anti-capitalism and José Martí's nationalism. The organization comprised intellectuals, students, representatives of radical sectors of the middle class, and workers. Its national-revolutionary program defended insurrection. The Communist Party and the National Working-Class Confederation of Cuba organized a strike that, apart from its particular demands, opposed both the Platt Amendment and the Treaty of Commercial Reciprocity with the United States signed in 1903.

SAVED THE CUBAN REVOLUTION

Batista violently repressed a major strike of sugar workers. But the peasant struggle nonetheless intensified. In Guantánamo, under the slogan "Land or Blood," some 5,000 families set an extraordinary example of resistance when they refused to be dispossessed from their lands. Cuba's liberal bourgeoisie, alarmed by the escalation of the labor and popular movements, enacted some reforms, including the abolition, in March 1934, of the Platt Amendment as an appendix of the Cuban constitution. In August, the United States and Cuba signed a new Treaty of Reciprocity; however, the new version still favored U.S. interests.

In early 1935, protests intensified, as did the government's repression. Things came to a head with a general strike that began March 6. The government declared a state of war, and the armed forces were ordered to shoot strikers. After the huge popular uprising was defeated, the government unleashed a wave of terror against the labor and revolutionary movements.

HISTORICAL SIGNIFICANCE OF THE REVOLUTION OF 1933

The revolutionary process of the 1930s was crushed in the short term. This period of Cuban history, however, saw extraordinary relevant shifts in the country's political culture. Anti-imperialist consciousness increased. Broad sectors of Cuba's people demonstrated a strong and vigorous opposition to the Cuban oligarchy and the threats of foreign intervention. The dominance of the traditional political parties was eroded. New organizations emerged, with new visions and perspectives. The necessity of alliances among workers, students, peasants, intellectuals, and professionals became evident. Revolutionary forces would need to mobilize the masses and employ a variety of militant strategies and tactics. This phase also exposed the indecisive, meek, and submissive nature of Cuba's bourgeoisie. The period after the fall of the 100 Days Government was fraught with good choices and errors, and its lessons proved instructive for the struggles to come.

THE 1940 CONSTITUTION

The defeat of the March 1935 strike demonstrated how far the regime

112   HOW THE WORKERS' PARLIAMENTS

was willing to go to repress any challenges. The press was censored, distribution of written propaganda was prohibited, the military interfered in the labor organizations and factories, and public offices dismissed anyone known as a regime opponent.

The popular movements began to respond, with the creation of new trade unions and other demonstrations of a renewed opposition. In late 1935, Batista opportunistically tried to convince Cubans that he would solve the problems in such critical areas as education, public health, and economic development. He granted amnesty to political prisoners and allowed exiles to return. The University Student Federation (FEU) was formed. (Its predecessor, the University Student Directorate, was dissolved in 1933.) Batista, always attentive to the signs emanating from Washington, enacted changes that reflected the U.S. reaction to international events, particularly the advance of fascism in Europe. Washington's stance toward Cuba and Latin America changed from outright military intervention to other, non-military ways to ensure that governments in the region supported U.S. interests.

Between 1938 and 1939, the rights of trade union organizations were recognized and opposition parties and organizations were legalized. On January 28, 1939, the *Confederación de Trabajadores de Cuba* (CTC) was established. This led to the reorganization of the Cuban trade union movement, with Lázaro Peña,[56] Jesús Menéndez,[57] Aracelio Iglesias,[58] and José María Pérez[59] among the most prominent working-class leaders.

During the government of Federico Laredo Brú,[60] from 1936 to 1940, a constituent assembly convened to draw up a new charter. It was replaced by the 1940 constitution, a document whose creation involved Cubans from various social origins and ideologies. Ricardo Alarcón, in his 2010 reflections on the constitution, noted:

> Those who drafted it, chosen in the middle of the prevailing limitations, would reflect, approximately, the confused, contradictory balance of the period. Machado's and Batista's supporters; communists and combatants of the 1930 Revolution; representatives of landowners and the bourgeoisie; and spokesmen of the labor

SAVED THE CUBAN REVOLUTION

movement and the peasants debated the main problems of the country for months, under the attentive eyes of the population....The result was one of the most advanced texts among those promulgated up to that moment in [Latin] America. It proscribed landowning and promoted State intervention in the economy; the exclusive dominance of the Republic over the subsoil; and it incorporated the main demands of the trade union movement; it established the creation of important institutions, such as the National Bank, the Court of Constitutional and Social Guarantees, and the Court of Accounts.[61]

The 1940 Constitution was approved during the outbreak of the Second World War (1939–1945), and the war's impact contributed to the inclusion of the most advanced political thinking of the time. As the text was being approved, workers' organizations organized demonstrations outside the Constituent Assembly to ensure that the constitution would be democratic and progressive. Once promulgated, on July 1, 1940, in Guáimaro, in the of Camagüey province, general elections were held, with two candidates for president: Fulgencio Batista and Ramón Grau San Martín.

FULGENCIO BATISTA: DEMAGOGY AND REPRESSION

Batista, who sought to play a leading role among those who wanted democratic transformation, presented a program of the so-called Democratic Socialist Coalition, which he led. The program included progressive demands, including that all laws must be consistent with the new constitution. Though opportunistic, Batista's embrace of reform led the Communist Revolutionary Union Party to support his candidacy. The decision to endorse Batista generated fierce polemics among members of the party, and many revolutionaries rejected it.

Batista was elected president. The new government marked the beginning of a period of constitutional normality, characterized by the primacy of civil and non-military institutions, the growing strength of the trade union movement, collaboration with democratic and antifascist forces during the Second World War, and, in 1945, Cuba joining

114 HOW THE WORKERS' PARLIAMENTS

the United Nations. With its influence increased through the trade union movement and the CTC, the Communist Revolutionary Union in 1944 changed its name to the Popular Socialist Party. The party had representation in the Cuban senate and House of Representatives. At the same time, Cuban youth, women, and peasants were building strong movements.

The country made some gains but significant challenges remained: administrative corruption, discrimination, and illiteracy. Prices began to rise because of the shortage of raw materials and products as a consequence of the world war. Speculation and the black market expanded, and discontent grew. Most of the laws derived from the 1940 constitution were not approved. In the social sphere, young male university and intermediate education students organized gangs that fraudulently obtained grades for its members, occupied positions without working, and engaged in violence.

Cubans rejected the government, electing Ramón Grau San Martín as president in 1944. His popularity grew in light of the country's situation and because of his participation in the government. Nevertheless, most members of the Congress, as well as mayors and council members, ended up in the hands of those who did not support true reforms. And Grau himself soon followed suit.

THE AUTHENTIC GOVERNMENTS

From 1933 to 1952, the *Partido Revolucionario Cubano—Auténtico* (Cuban Revolutionary Party—Authentic) was Cuba's dominant political party. Born in the 1933 nationalist revolution, in 1934 it comprised many of the same persons who had overthrown many in the Machado dictatorship. Its candidate, Ramón Grau San Martín, served two terms as Cuba's president, 1933–34 and 1944–48. The first two years saw the adoption of measures to develop the country and improve the lives of the Cuban people. They included the approval of the sugar differential. In the sugarcane harvest of 1945, 250,000 tons were retained for sale to Latin American countries at 7 cents per pound, whereas the United States paid 3.67 cents. The differential was used to subsidize food and to defray the costs of public works. Based on that experience, the workers proposed a new differential that would be based on the increased price the United States paid for Cuban sugar, in a proportionate rate to what Cuba paid for imported U.S. products. A commission was created to discuss the subject in Washington with respect to the 1945–46 sugarcane harvest. Despite U.S. resistance, a guarantee clause stipulated that price variations be calculated every three months.

After 1946, however, the Grau government became one of the most corrupt in Cuban history. President Grau permitted impunity, corruption, and gangsterism. His administration relinquished the sugar differential and rolled back achievements that benefited workers. Old vices linked to the management of public goods expanded; numerous government functionaries amassed huge fortunes and engaged in business fraud. Grau protected and supported the most notorious characters, among them his closest collaborators.

In the second Authentic government, under President Carlos Prío Socarrás (1948–52), many of the same evils persisted: administrative corruption; mismanagement of public funds; the fostering of so-called action groups, gangster-like organizations whose leaders held important positions in the police corps, military intelligence, and state organizations. The trade union movement was violently attacked, to dismember it and expel communists from its ranks. Mujalism, a term denoting corrupt, anti-communist trade unionism, was consolidated.[62]

By the early 1950s, the economy had stalled. It experienced increased U.S. investment in non-sugar sectors, misuse of public funds, and negative budgetary and tax-related practices. Production needed to be diversified and communication routes improved. Agrarian reform, development of national industry, and expansion into new international markets—all were urgent priorities.

Social ills proliferated. Nine thousand teachers were unemployed; illiteracy rose to 23 percent; 800,000 children, especially in the countryside, did not attend school; the child mortality rate was 60 for every 1,000 born and 42.2 in children under five years of age. The average life expectancy was only 55 years. Fifty-nine percent of Cuban

116 HOW THE WORKERS' PARLIAMENTS

physicians practiced in Havana. Unemployment affected 600,000 workers—nearly 25 percent of the economically active population—during the eight months when sugarcane was not being harvested; even during the harvest season, unemployment stood at 10 to 12 percent. Prostitution, gambling, begging; children shining shoes or selling newspapers to survive; and handicapped people living in the streets and dependent on public charity all became common features of everyday life.

EDUARDO CHIBÁS: DECENCY VERSUS MONEY

On May 15, 1947, Eduardo Chibás, a senator since 1944, founded the *Partido Ortodoxo* (Orthodox Party), in response to the corruption of the Authentic Party government. The Orthodox program had a progressive character based on national sovereignty, economic independence, diversified agriculture, elimination of large agricultural estates, industrial development, and nationalization of public services. The party opposed corruption, upheld social justice, and defended workers.

From 1943 to 1951, Chibás used his popular weekly radio program to denounce the state's corruption. He called for leaders who would be committed to building a new Cuba and who demonstrated honesty and rectitude. In *Conversaciones con el líder histórico de la Revolución cubana* (Talks with the Historic Leader of the Cuban Revolution), Fidel Castro described Chibás as a combative and honest leader who was genuinely opposed to corruption and vice.[63] But in the 1950 electoral campaign, Chibás denounced Minister of Education Aureliano Sánchez Arango, claiming that he owned estates in Guatemala. The government, declaring this charge a calumny, demanded that he produce evidence. He promised to do so, but when he could not, he shot himself at the end of his last radio program. He died eleven days later, on August 16, 1951.

THE COUP OF MARCH 10, 1952

In the presidential elections scheduled for June 1, 1952, three parties

SAVED THE CUBAN REVOLUTION 117

were to present candidates: Carlos Hevia, from the Authentic Party; Fulgencio Batista, from the Unitary Action Party; and Roberto Agramonte, from the Orthodox Party. Although Agramonte held some conservative positions, he was the only candidate who represented change; he was seen as continuing Eduardo Chibás's leadership. All polling proclaimed him the winner. For the United States, however, neither the Authentic nor the Orthodox parties were acceptable; only Batista would protect its interests. Batista, the so-called strongman, had no chance of being elected. So, on March 10, 1952, just seven months after Chibás's death and three months before the presidential elections, he overthrew Carlos Prío Socarrás, who offered no resistance and fled the country without resigning his position.

It was the beginning of a phase of open and brutal terror.

On March 27, 1952, the United States officially acknowledged Batista's regime; in July, Washington signed a military agreement with Havana. The general would ruthlessly repress opposition, particularly the student population, symbolized by the murder of Rubén Batista in January 1953.[64] Batista's coup was widely condemned. A young lawyer named Fidel Castro Ruz, who had been a prominent student activist, published an article that denounced Batista, on March 14, 1952.

The traditional political parties were in a profound crisis; some supported Batista, others dissolved; others, including the Orthodox Party, called for resistance, citing the authority of the Cuban Constitution. The official trade union movement offered its services to Batista, but other currents in the labor movement condemned the Batista regime and organized protests. Still, the repression didn't inspire a massive, general revolt.

The Batista dictatorship abolished the 1940 constitution and its guarantees and dissolved the Congress, replacing it with a so-called Consultative Council. General elections were indefinitely postponed; mayors and council members were dismissed and replaced by others acceptable to the dictatorship. Radio broadcasts of a political nature were suppressed; television programs were cancelled; all public demonstrations were forbidden. The Committee to Investigate Communist

118 HOW THE WORKERS' PARLIAMENTS

Activities was created not only to suppress communism but any popular expression of dissent or opposition to the regime.

The dictatorship increased military spending as Cubans' cost of living rose and their salaries fell. The theft of lands by landowners was legitimized. The regime signed numerous agreements with the United States that favored U.S. enterprises in Cuba, thereby reinforcing Cuba's economic subservience to the United States.

POPULAR REPUDIATION GROWS

Resistance to the Batista regime increased; the opposition, however, could not agree on how to fight it. The student movement organized protests that often evoked milestones of Cuban history. The centenary of José Martí's birth in January 1953 served as an occasion to express their rejection and defiance of the regime. In the early hours of January 27, the Federation of University Students organized a procession from the University of Havana to Fragua Martiana (Martí's Forge).[65] Participants, who included youth and revolutionary organizations, as well as average Cubans, carried lighted torches. This stunning and well-organized event was led by young men and women of the emerging movement led by Fidel Castro and Abel Santamaría.[66] From its ranks would come the revolutionaries who, on July 26, 1953, would profoundly change Cuban history.

The movement was composed mainly of young men and women from the Orthodox Party. Organized in cells comprising six to twelve members, each cell with a leader, they prepared for combat, in target practice classes, assembling and stripping weapons, and also training in self-defense and tactical exercises. Beginning in March 1953, they organized actions for Santiago de Cuba and Bayamo. They bought weapons and secured lodging in both places. From July 20 to 23, the combatants mobilized; on July 24, they departed from Havana, a force of 160 men and women.

THE ASSAULTS OF JULY 26, 1953

The July 26, 1953, assaults on two fortresses, the Moncada in Santiago

SAVED THE CUBAN REVOLUTION 119

de Cuba and the Carlos Manuel de Céspedes in Bayamo, are two of the most inspiring events of Cuban revolutionary history.

The plan was to assault the Moncada barracks, the main provincial garrison of Batista's troops, and seize the adjacent Palace of Justice, a nearby hospital, and a radio station. The goal was to incite a popular uprising, with the hope that the army would join and force Batista from power. "Even if it failed," Fidel noted, "it would be heroic and have symbolic value." The Moncada assailants comprised three groups: the first, led by Abel Santamaría, was to seize the part of the hospital adjacent to the fortress barracks. The second, led by Raúl Castro, would take the Palace of Justice; and the third, led by Fidel Castro, would take the control station, the General Staff, with eight to nine men; the rest would occupy the barracks.

The attack began at 5:15 in the morning; the sun had already risen in the east. The Moncada assailants arrived in ten to twelve cars. Those in the first car, Ramiro Valdés,[67] Jesús Montané,[68] Renato Guitart,[69] among others, neutralized the control station guards, seizing their weapons. However, the regime, capitalizing on the revolutionaries' disorganization, recovered from the surprise attack and defended its positions. Faced with more than 1,000 heavily armed regime soldiers, the revolutionaries had no choice but to withdraw. Their casualties were light; only eight fighters were killed and twelve injured, but another fifty-six were later tracked down and killed. (The simultaneous attack on the Carlos Manuel de Cespedes barracks in Bayamo also failed.)

Once the decision to withdraw had been made, the insurgents returned to the small farm in Siboney from which they had departed for the assault in order to reorganize. A group of nineteen left with Fidel Castro to take refuge in the Sierra Maestra, evading Batista's soldiers. Fidel and two comrades advanced along the coast, with the purpose of crossing the bay toward the mountains. Exhausted, they decided to sleep in a *varaentierra* (rustic shack), where they were surprised by a military patrol. Lieutenant Pedro Sarría, who led the patrol that captured them, prevented their assassination. According to Fidel, Sarria said, "Do not shoot, ideas are not to be killed!"[70]

"CONDEMN ME, IT DOESN'T MATTER, HISTORY WILL ABSOLVE ME"

The trial of the participants in the events of July 26 began September 21, 1953, in the Eastern Criminal Court.

Marta Rojas, a young journalist, covered the trial. She reported that Fidel, along with Haydée Santamaría[71] and Melba Hernández,[72] entered the courtroom in handcuffs. Once inside, he raised his arms and protested that a defendant should not be handcuffed. The handcuffs were removed. That was his first victory. As an attorney, he requested to be allowed to represent himself in court, a common practice in Cuba at the time. His request was accepted, but first he was subjected to questioning by the court. His responses convincingly refuted the lies in the official reports. He declared himself the organizer of the movement that carried out the July 26 actions and proclaimed José Martí as their intellectual author.

He indignantly rebutted the public prosecutor's accusation that the revolutionaries had cruelly murdered soldiers, highlighting the exemplary behavior of the comrades who had seized the Palace of Justice and captured its security guards. The revolutionaries' captives were unharmed, but the regime's soldiers tortured and murdered many of the revolutionaries they detained. He also explained that the money for the assaults came from Cubans who believed that armed struggle was the only way to radically transform their country.

After two hours of the court's questions, the examination concluded. Now, wearing his lawyer's robe, Fidel moved to the jurists' platform. He questioned his comrades, the leaders of the opposition political parties who also were on trial, the military officers, the expert ballistic witnesses, and the forensic physicians. Their answers revealed the horrendous crimes that Batista's soldiers committed immediately after the assault. What was exposed in court that day dealt a powerful blow to Batista's dictatorship and the military men who obeyed his orders to torture and murder the prisoners.

The revelations were so stunning that the dictatorship ordered the court to remove Doctor of Law Fidel Castro from the trial. The regime

SAVED THE CUBAN REVOLUTION

even planned to assassinate him if necessary. He would be allowed to escape. And then he would be shot in the back. But instead, the regime had a physician certify that he was too ill to return to court. The trial continued with the other defendants testifying in his absence. They testified to the orgy of horror and death that consumed the young men and women who participated in the heroic events of July 26, 1953, in Santiago de Cuba and Bayamo.

When the first phase of the trial ended, the revolutionaries were sentenced to imprisonment. The politicians who had been implicated in the cause were found not guilty.

On October 16, 1953, in a nursing ward of Saturnino Lora Hospital, the trial against the main defendant, Fidel Castro Ruz, began. He testified that soldiers had massacred prisoners (they were ordered to kill ten revolutionaries for every soldier killed in the attacks) and tortured them. He told how soldiers had dragged wounded revolutionaries— whom they had already tortured— from their hospital beds, bound and gagged them, and then killed them in remote locations. Many were forced to dig their own graves; others were buried alive, their hands tied behind their backs. He denounced the violation of his rights as both a prisoner and an attorney; he was not permitted any law books or other books he might consult for his defense, including the works of Jose Martí.

He spoke about Cuba's fundamental problems: land, industrialization, housing, unemployment, education. and health. Then, he concluded, "As for me, I know prison will be hard as it has never been to anyone, full of threats, of despicable and cowardly cruelty. But I do not fear it, as I do not fear the fury of the wicked tyrant who snatched away the lives of seventy brothers of mine. Condemn me, it doesn't matter, history will absolve me."

Minutes after Fidel finished speaking, the guilty verdict was announced, and he was sentenced to prison.

The July 26 assaults were military failures. Still, they had the historic value of opening up a path to armed insurrection against the dictatorship. A new revolutionary vanguard emerged, one that would make extraordinary sacrifices for the emancipation the Cuban people longed for.

122 HOW THE WORKERS' PARLIAMENTS

Imprisoned on Isla de Pinos, Castro and his comrades founded an "academy" they named for Abel Santamaría and a library named for the poet Raúl Gómez García. They studied mathematics, history, Spanish, English, and Marx's *Capital*. They received books from family and friends. They received items of great value from the outside, but, at the same time, indications emanated from jail. In the center of hollowed-out cigars, at the bottom of packets of matches, in small letters, they hid and sent their messages. In this way, they evaded the prison censorship.

THE RELEASE OF THE "MONCADISTS"

The families of prisoners began to agitate for their release, with mothers taking a prominent role. Little by little, the campaign—directed by Fidel from prison—spread throughout the country. The Pro-Amnesty Committee of Relatives of Political Prisoners influenced and mobilized popular opinion in favor of the prisoners' release. Under the leadership of José Antonio Echeverria and Fructuoso Rodríguez, the University Student Federation joined the campaign for the release of the Moncadists and of all imprisoned revolutionaries.

The pressure paid off. On May 15, 1955, the prisoners were released. In a press conference from the Isla de Pinos Hotel, Fidel called the amnesty a great victory for the Cuban people. He also affirmed that the struggle against the dictatorship would go on. A month later, a new phase of the Cuban Revolution was initiated with the founding of the *Movimiento 26 de Julio* (July 26 Movement).

THE *GRANMA*

Given the impossibility of deposing Batista through legal means, Fidel Castro left Cuba for Mexico on July 7, 1955, to organize an armed insurrection. In Mexico, he met the Argentinian physician and revolutionary Ernesto "Che" Guevara. Guevara had fled Guatemala to escape the repression by the regime that the United States imposed after the overthrow of the government of Jacobo Arbenz.[73] Fidel described the encounter in an interview with the Spanish journalist

SAVED THE CUBAN REVOLUTION

Ignacio Ramonet.[74] In an April 1958 interview from Sierra Maestra with the Argentine journalist Jorge Ricardo Masetti, Che recalled, "I talked to Fidel the whole night. And at dawn, I was already the doctor for the future expedition."[75]

From Mexico, Fidel traveled to the United States. On his visits to several cities, he met with exiled revolutionaries. Funds raised from thousands of Cubans enabled them to acquire houses, uniforms, equipment, and weapons. Donations from Cuba were combined with those from the patriotic clubs in exile and Mexican friends. The revolutionaries established their first camp and began military training. They faced many setbacks. Cuba's Mexican embassy, including agents of Batista's Military Intelligence Service, bribed Mexican authorities to pursue the exiled revolutionaries. The police arrested many of them, including Fidel. Several houses and the camp were raided and weapons were seized. Although the raids cost the revolutionaries time and resources obtained with great sacrifice, they didn't abandon their plans. Instead, they sought different locations, more weapons, and other resources. They also improved their security measures.

In Delaware, the revolutionaries purchased a ship to bring an expedition to Cuba, but they could not obtain an exit permit. This cost them $8,000. They acquired an old recreational yacht, the *Granma*.

In Mexico, the revolutionaries held critical meetings, including one between Fidel and Frank País, who, though barely twenty-two years old, impressed Castro with his intelligence, courage, organizational abilities, and moral and ideological qualities.[76] After the March 10, 1952, coup, País declared his opposition to the regime. He published articles denouncing the regime and joined the National Revolutionary Movement led by Rafael García Bárcena.[77] País established links with another organization, *Acción Nacional Liberadora* (National Liberation Action/ANL) but later broke with it to form *Acción Revolucionaria Oriental* (Eastern Revolutionary Action/ARO). Extended to other provinces, it was renamed *Acción Nacional Revolucionaria* (National Revolutionary Action/ANR). The ANR obtained dynamite and staged explosions, the first acts of sabotage against the regime. When Fidel founded the July 26 Movement, País

124   HOW THE WORKERS' PARLIAMENTS

put himself under his command as a combatant and handed over his entire organization to him. País was then appointed to lead the movement's activities in Oriente province.

José Antonio Echeverría, president of the FEU, also went to Mexico. In 1955, he and several comrades organized the Revolutionary Directorate, which, under the direction of the FEU, attracted the most radical students and other youth. The meeting of the July 26 Movement and the Revolutionary Directorate leaders in Mexico, on August 29, 1956, produced the "Letter of Mexico." This document emphasized united efforts to overthrow the dictatorship and to achieve the Revolution's goals: social justice, freedom, and democracy. The letter was published September 1, 1956.

Fidel also met with Flavio Bravo of the Popular Socialist Party.[78] They agreed on strategic objectives but differed over when to begin the insurrection against the dictatorship. The Popular Socialist Party believed that it wasn't feasible to launch a military campaign before December 31. The party also argued that armed insurrection should be accompanied by a militant strike by sugar workers. But a strike could not take place until the sugarcane harvest began, so the socialists recommended delaying the expedition's departure for thirty to forty days.

While acknowledging the soundness of the party's arguments, Fidel nonetheless insisted that there was no other alternative but to initiate the fight in Cuba. In Mexico, the revolutionaries were being persecuted and their weapons confiscated. They risked losing everything if the operation was postponed.

On November 25, 1956, at 1:30 a.m., the *Granma*, with its lights off and moving slowly, and unauthorized to sail because of bad weather, weighed anchor from Veracruz, heading toward the Gulf of Mexico and the Caribbean. Low on fuel and food, the *Granma* entered the Niquero Canal and then ran aground two kilometers from Las Coloradas Beach, at the northeast of Cabo Cruz. This swampy area, which extended inland, was not the planned disembarkation point. It was 6:00 a.m., December 2, 1956.

THE NOVEMBER 30 UPRISING IN SANTIAGO DE CUBA

The disembarkation did not coincide with the uprising of Santiago de Cuba, as Fidel Castro and Frank País had planned during their Mexico meeting. The insurrection began an hour later. The revolutionaries' cries of "Long live Fidel!" "Long live the Revolution!" "Down with Batista!" were echoed by the people of Santiago de Cuba, who were seeing for the first time the olive-green uniforms and the red and black armbands of the July 26 Movement.

The targets included the headquarters of the National Police, the Maritime Police, where the revolutionaries took prisoners and weapons, a gunsmith's shop, and the Moncada fortress. (The Moncada attack, however, was not carried out.) By noon, Batista's forces were reinforced; its superior numbers and weaponry led Frank País to call for withdrawal. Three valued young fighters gave their lives that day: Otto Parellada,[79] Tony Alomá,[80] and Pepito Tey.[81]

The events of November 30 were met with ferocious persecution by the dictatorship of the people of Santiago. They had shown their solidarity with the revolutionaries by opening their doors to them. They helped the wounded, hid weapons and uniforms, and warned about the army's movements. The wounded were protected, and the unhurt assailants went underground.

THE NATIONAL LIBERATION WAR

Three days later, on December 5, regime aircraft attacked the revolutionaries' camp at Alegría de Pío. Dispersed from the camp, some were killed or captured, while others headed for Sierra Maestra. Aided by the network of peasants organized by Frank País and Celia Sánchez, they managed to regroup.[82]

On December 16, Fidel and two members of the expedition arrived in Vicana Arriba, in the foothills of Sierra Maestra. They reached it after a long, arduous trek without food or water. On December 18, a peasant informed Fidel that his brother Raúl likely was in the area. At midnight, in Cinco Palmas, they met, embracing each other with deep

126 HOW THE WORKERS' PARLIAMENTS

emotion. "How many rifles did you bring?" Fidel asked. "Five," said Raúl. Fidel replied, "And with the two I have, seven! Now we win the war!"

On December 21, they were fifteen, along with the peasants who joined them. Four days later, they marched deep into Sierra Maestra. They formed the main nucleus of what would become the *Ejército Rebelde* (Rebel Army), whose first fight was simply to survive.

In the cities, actions against the dictatorship were gestating. Batista's police seized guns, uniforms, and armbands of the July 26 Movement and detained thousands. After revolutionaries attacked an ammunition dump, Batista retaliated. Between December 23 and 26, the dictatorship killed twenty-three people, a slaughter that would be sadly remembered as *Pascuas Sangrientas* (Bloody Christmas).

After Alegría de Pío, the regime ferociously pursued the guerrillas. They nonetheless carried out some successful attacks, including an assault on January 17, 1957, on the La Plata Fortress. The victory, after only forty minutes of fighting, had both military and symbolic significance for the army. The rebel army was present in the eastern mountains.

On February 17, the *New York Times* reporter Hebert Matthews interviewed Fidel. Matthews's reporting informed the world about the insurrection brewing in Sierra Maestra and that its leader, Fidel Castro, was alive and fighting. That same day, the National Directorate of the July 26 Movement met in Sierra Maestra to plan further actions.

The fight against the Batista dictatorship was gaining ground. Clandestine actions increased in cities and towns, involving broad segments of the population, including youth. Money, clothes, food, and medicine were collected and sent to the guerrillas.

On March 13, the Revolutionary Directorate, led by José Antonio Echeverrería, attacked the Presidential Palace. They intended to execute Batista and to incite an armed insurrection in Havana. Their plans included seizing the Radio Reloj station and setting up an operational center at the University of Havana. From there, they would distribute weapons to the people.

Only a few of the fifty revolutionaries who attacked the Presidential

SAVED THE CUBAN REVOLUTION

Palace penetrated the building. Some reached the second story before the garrison's snipers positioned on the top floor controlled the corridors. They reached Batista's office, but the tyrant had already fled. José Antonio Echeverrería estimated that the revolutionaries could occupy Radio Reloj for only three minutes, so he prepared a brief speech, which he finished right on time. He left the station unharmed, but on the way to the University of Havana, he was killed in a shootout with Batista's police. Twenty-five young revolutionaries died in that action. Besides those who died in the events of March 13, four other participants were assassinated on April 20: Fructuoso Rodríguez,[83] Juan Pedro Carbó,[84] José Machado,[85] and Joe Westbrook.[86]

In March, the first reinforcement of men sent from the plains had arrived in Sierra Maestra. On May 28, the *guerrilleros* (guerrilla combatants) attacked the Uvero fortress; the battle lasted almost three hours.[87] The guerrillas seized guns, projectiles, uniforms, and other military supplies. They also took prisoners. By July, the rebel army was consolidated in Sierra Maestra. Fidel Castro led Column No. 1, *José Martí*, while Che Guevara was commander of Column 4. Guevara's column began operations in Pico Turquino, in the El Hombrito zone. Sometimes the two columns acted independently, at others, together.

On July 30, in the streets of Santiago de Cuba, Frank País and Raúl Pujol[88] were killed. The news spread all over Cuba, despite official censorship. A spontaneous general strike broke out in Oriente and spread to other provinces. On September 5, Authentic Party members joined the July 26 Movement in a plot to stage multiple coordinated attacks on Havana military headquarters. However, they failed to inform their comrades at Cayo Loco naval station in Cienfuegos that the date of the uprising had been postponed. Unaware of the change in plans, the Cayo Loco forces acted alone and were quickly defeated.

Although the action failed, it had significant repercussions. It likely influenced the United States to impose an embargo on Batista's regime six months later. The thwarted revolt led Batista to purge the military, with many air force officers imprisoned for rebellion and treason. Many others were dishonorably discharged. Batista perceived the air force as disloyal, further eroding the morale of the Cuban armed forces.

In 1958, the guerrillas continued to build their forces in Sierra Maestra. Meanwhile, anti-Batista activity intensified in the cities. In Havana, on February 23, July 26 Movement members kidnapped Juan Manuel Fangio, an Argentine auto racing champion who was in Cuba to participate in a race. The kidnapping brought international attention to the struggle against the Batista dictatorship. On February 24, Radio Rebelde station began broadcasting from Sierra Maestra. In March, three new fronts were formed: the Frank País Second Eastern Front, under Raúl Castro's command; the Dr. Mario Muñoz Monroy Third Eastern Front, led by Juan Almeida Bosque;[89] and Column 7, commanded by Crescencio Pérez.[90] On March 31, a force led by Camilo Cienfuegos left for an action in the Cauto River plains.[91]

The students' Revolutionary Directorate and the Popular Socialist Party joined the armed struggle. The Directorate had organized the Second National Front of Escambray, led by Eloy Gutiérrez Menoyo.[92] But its leadership was unreliable, and its guerrillas committed abuses against peasants. Faure Chomón, General Secretary of the Directorate, was sent to reinforce the Escambray front.

The Popular Socialist Party began operations in the Las Villas province. Félix Torres organized PSP and July 26 Movement members into an armed detail that carried out numerous actions.[93]

While the armed struggle was intensifying in the mountains and the cities, in the electoral field the traditional political parties and the institutions of the bourgeoisie sought conciliation. Batista called for new elections. On March 1, the Catholic Church hierarchy advocated a government of national unity that would include representatives of the dictatorship, with Batista at its head. An entity called Commission of National Concord was created. Fidel Castro, from Sierra Maestra, adamantly rejected this shady deal. On March 12, in Sierra Maestra, Fidel Castro and Faustino Pérez,[94] a July 26 Movement leader, authorized a mass strike.

In late 1957, July 26 Movement trade union leaders organized the *Frente Obrero Nacional* (National Labor Front/FON). It was tasked with organizing the strike, while the Movement of Civic Resistance would deal with the professional sectors and the National Student Front of the

SAVED THE CUBAN REVOLUTION 129

July 26 Movement. Fidel Castro called on FON to coordinate with all anti-Batista labor organizations. On April 9, 1958, two radio stations announced the strike. There were actions in Havana and elsewhere, but they failed to achieve their goal of paralyzing the country. Fidel analyzed in detail the causes of the failure and asserted that the errors would not be repeated. The revolution had lost a battle, but not the war.[95]

On May 3, 1958, the July 26 Movement's directorate met in Sierra Maestra to analyze the strike's failure.[96] They agreed that the Directorate should be restructured. They designated Fidel as general secretary of the movement and commander in chief of all forces. Extending the armed struggle would be the main strategy, with a mass strike a last resort.

As two writers later recalled, "The repression unleased by the tyranny after the failed general strike [was] aimed mainly at the clandestine combatants in the cities. . . . The high-ranking officers of the tyranny did not hide their euphoria; they soon falsely proclaimed the end of the revolutionary movement on all fronts, and intoxicated with their partial successes, they thought it was the appropriate time for a coup de grâce against what they considered the last redoubt of the revolutionary movement: Sierra Maestra."[97]

On May 25, 1958, the dictatorship launched an offensive to take the General Command of the Rebel Army and thereby inflict a fatal blow on the Revolution. Most of Batista's forces headed for the Sierra Maestra foothills, where they encountered fierce resistance from the revolutionaries, who knew the terrain well. The enemy troops dropped napalm and high-powered explosives and machine-gunned hamlets in Sierra Maestra.

The guerrillas, under Fidel Castro's leadership, defeated Batista's forces. With this victory, the rebel forces gained the strategic advantage. In the Battle of Jigüe, an entire battalion of Batista's forces was surrounded and defeated. Batista had mobilized some 10,000 troops from the army, air force, navy, rural guard, the police, and paramilitary forces. The rebel army, which began operations with only about 200, compensated for its numerical inferiority with more astute strategy and greater intelligence, courage, and tenacity.

130 HOW THE WORKERS' PARLIAMENTS

With its May offensive having failed, Batista's army went on the defense from fortresses in towns and cities. But the dictatorship's collapse nonetheless accelerated.

The rebel army inflicted more than a thousand casualties and took more than four-hundred prisoners, who were handed over to the International Red Cross. The revolutionaries also seized huge numbers of weapons and equipment. In thirty-five days, the revolutionaries drove out Batista's forces from Sierra Maestra. Their defeat created the conditions for the rebel army's final offensive. Commander in Chief Fidel Castro conceived a strategy with economic, political, and military aspects. Militarily, his idea was to make eastern Cuba a great battlefield and then extend the conflict to the rest of the country.

He planned two military campaigns: one in the east, under his command, was to break up the regime's garrisons, destroy its communications, occupy the most important towns and cities, and seize Santiago de Cuba. Che Guevara would lead a second campaign in Las Villas, in collaboration with other forces in the area. This force was to impede regime troops from moving eastward or withdrawing to the west.

In August, Column No. 2, Antonio Maceo, led by Camilo Cienfuegos, and Column No. 8, Ciro Redondo, commanded by Che, left Sierra Maestra for the plains. The combatants endured illness, hunger, and thirst. They traveled by foot—sometimes barefoot—over muddy roads and under attack by Batista's army and air force. In early October, the two columns reached Las Villas, where conditions were more favorable. All guerrilla fighters in the area were organized under the rebel army's command.

Cienfuegos's column was to establish a permanent front in Pinar del Río, the farthest west province. But after assessing the situation in Las Villas, in the center of the country, Fidel Castro ordered him to continue operations in its northern areas.

On December 1, the unity of all revolutionary forces was sealed with the Pedrero Pact, signed by leaders of the July 26 Movement, the Revolutionary Directorate, and the Popular Socialist Party.

In Las Villas, the revolutionaries attacked military convoys and their

SAVED THE CUBAN REVOLUTION 131

reinforcements and blew up bridges, as part of the strategy to advance on and take control of Santa Clara. On December 28, the rebel forces entered the city, supported by clandestine fighters, who acted as guides. The population supported the combatants in various ways, including barricading city streets, while Batista's forces attacked the city from the air. The revolutionaries derailed and attacked one of the regime's armored trains; its troops surrendered.

On December 30, all of Santa Clara was fighting and important targets were falling into rebel hands. The air force attacks continued the next day, but the dictatorship's tanks and infantry left their regiment for the last time. Conditions were propitious for the revolutionaries to encircle and attack the Yaguajay fortress. When it was surrendered, Camilo Cienfuegos was free to assist Che in the final effort. On January 1, 1959, the rebel army occupied Santa Clara. The dictatorship's military chief fled, and twelve days later, unconditionally surrendered. The second and the third columns took towns and cities in their operation zones and revolutionary forces advanced toward Santiago de Cuba. Desertions from Batista's armed forces increased, while some soldiers joined the rebels.

In view of the imminent collapse of the dictatorship, representatives of the Cuban bourgeoisie, the military, and the U.S. government pressured Batista to resign, in the hope that his departure would delay or prevent the revolutionaries' victory. The U.S. ambassador announced that his government would withdraw its support of Batista. On December 28, Fidel Castro and General Eulogio Cantillo met in the ruins of the Oriente sugar mill, at Cantillo's request.[98] Fidel argued that the soldiers were victims of the regime, which had constantly deceived them. He made it clear that he would never accept any settlement that allowed Batista to escape. He demanded the handover of war criminals. He asserted that the July 26 Movement and the Cuban people would never support a military junta to replace Batista.

It was established in the meeting between Castro and Cantillo that the uprising would occur at 3:00 p.m. on December 31. The support of the armed forces for the revolutionary movement would be unconditional. The Santiago de Cuba garrison would rise up and,

132   HOW THE WORKERS' PARLIAMENTS

immediately afterward, several rebel columns would enter the city. Troops that had fought honorably and had not committed atrocities would be invited to join the revolutionary movement. The army's tanks would be put at the disposal of the rebel forces. An armored column would advance toward Havana where the dictatorship continued to inflict violent repression.

Cantillo, however, did not abide by the agreements.

On December 30, fighting ended in Maffo, a town equidistant from Bayamo and Santiago de Cuba, after twenty days. Maffo was the last town that Batista's army controlled. Soldiers took shelter in warehouses and dug underground tunnels. Nothing they did could halt the rebel forces, who seized huge numbers of weapons. This decisive victory made it possible for the revolutionaries to advance on Santiago de Cuba.

On December 31, Fidel went on Radio Rebelde to announce the dictatorship's imminent defeat. On January 1, Batista handed over the leadership of the armed forces to Eulogio Cantillo, resigned as president, and fled the country with his closest collaborators. Cantillo, backed by the U.S. embassy, designated Carlos M. Piedra as provisional president.[99]

Radio Rebelde informed the people that Batista had fled the country. General Cantillo assumed command of the military junta. The rebel leadership issued calls to stay alert in those decisive moments for the destiny of the homeland, because the long and difficult battle fought could have no other end but the triumph of the Revolution, and he called the people to be ready for declaring a general strike, preventing the escape of the assassins, demanding the immediate release of the political prisoners and not accepting any military junta.

On Radio Rebelde, Fidel ordered rebel army commanders to keep fighting and called on the Cuban people to rise up in a general strike: "Revolution, Yes. No to a military coup behind the people's and the Revolution's back. No, because [this] would only prolong the war." He drew up the final strategy for entering Santiago de Cuba and ordered the columns commanded by Cienfuegos and Guevara to continue marching toward Havana.

THE TRIUMPH OF THE REVOLUTION

On January 1, 1959, rebel forces led by Fidel, Raúl Castro, and Juan Almeida advanced on Santiago de Cuba. The Moncada fortress surrendered unconditionally. At 11:00 that night, Fidel announced the revolutionary triumph. He condemned the attempted military coup and denounced Cantillo's betrayals. He stated that Manuel Urrutia Lleó, a judge, would become the provisional president of the Republic.[100] In Havana, General Cantillo, in a new maneuver, handed the leadership of the army to Colonel Ramón Barquín, but this attempt to halt the Revolution's victory was frustrated.[101] A general strike broke out. The rebels seized fortresses and arrested Batista henchmen who had not escaped and would later be put on trial. Towns and cities were in the hands of the revolutionaries. The Revolution had triumphed.

On January 2, Fidel, leading a Freedom Caravan, departed Santiago de Cuba. Huge crowds greeted them at every point on their journey to Havana. On January 8, they arrived in the capital. At the Presidential Palace, Fidel, speaking to the crowd that had gathered, said that the general strike had been decisive in overthrowing the dictatorship. In the aftermath of the revolutionary victory, he visited places, talked to the people, met with representatives of the press, gave speeches, and went to Guanajay, in Artemisa, the birthplace of many of the July 26, 1953, martyrs. In Pinar del Río, he addressed the people, explaining the main tasks ahead. On January 22, he met with representatives of foreign media to refute the distorted coverage of the trials and executions of Batista's men who had committed crimes against the people.

CUBA TRANSFORMS ITSELF

The triumph of the Cuban Revolution signaled the beginning of profound changes in the country's economic, political, and social life. An old society was dying, while another was being born.

The revolutionary government moved quickly to bury the old order and bring the new one to life. It confiscated assets embezzled under the Batista regime. Workers who had been fired from their jobs were reinstated. The new government promulgated the First Law of Agrarian Reform and the Law of Urban Reform, which gave tenants ownership of their residences. The institutions of the neocolonial political system, its repressive bodies and political parties, were dismantled. The dictatorship's most notorious war criminals, informers, and torturers were put on trial. Public administration was reorganized.

These actions generated broad popular support. But a confrontation was brewing between the revolutionary government and sectors of the old regime that had lost economic and political power. They felt threatened by the Revolution's plans to establish new structures and social relations.

When it became evident that Batista's fall was inevitable, the United States made last-minute efforts to back a third force that would prevent the July 26 Movement from taking power. These efforts came to naught. On January 7, the United States officially recognized Cuba's new government. But at the same time, it planned to prevent the consolidation of the Revolution and to protect its interests in Cuba. The first hostile act was to grant political asylum to officials of the Batista dictatorship. U.S. media relentlessly attacked the Revolution for trying and sentencing to death regime members who had been responsible for atrocities they committed.

After the revolutionary government came to power on January 1, 1959, Fidel Castro made overtures to the United States, but he was rebuffed by the Eisenhower administration. In March, the United States already had a plan to overthrow his government. The "Covert Action Program Against the Castro Regime" called for "the creation of a responsible, appealing and unified Cuban opposition to the Castro regime, publicly declared as such and therefore necessarily located outside of Cuba."[102] The U.S.-sponsored counterrevolution would require "a powerful propaganda offensive" and "the creation of a covert intelligence and action organization within Cuba which will be responsive to the orders and directions of the 'exile' opposition." To carry out the program, the United States would prepare "an adequate paramilitary force outside of Cuba, together with mechanisms for the necessary logistic support of covert military operations on the Island."[103]

From January to October 1960, the U.S. government and Cuba clashed over oil, sugar, and the nationalization of U.S. and other foreign companies. In July, the United States reduced its import quota of Cuban sugar, but the Soviet Union agreed to purchase the sugar. In October, the United States refused to export oil to Cuba, leaving Cuba reliant on Soviet crude oil, which the three American companies in Cuba refused to refine. Cuba then nationalized the American-owned oil refineries. The Eisenhower administration then imposed the first U.S. trade embargo, prohibiting the sale of any products to Cuba except food and medicine. Cuba subsequently nationalized all American businesses and most privately owned American properties.

The U.S. economic warfare against revolutionary Cuba was accompanied by counterrevolutionary activities, first by elements of the Batista regime, then terrorist attacks on Cuba's coasts and fishing vessels, as well as other acts of sabotage undertaken with the CIA's involvement. On March 4, 1960, an explosion on the *La Coubre* steamship killed more than a hundred. On April 13, 1961, El Encanto, a Havana department store, was burned down, causing the death of a woman worker and several injuries.

PLAYA GIRÓN (BAY OF PIGS)

In January 1961, President John F. Kennedy authorized Operation Pluto, which would land a Cuban exile force on the coast of Trinidad, Cuba, between the Escambray Mountains and Cuba's southern shores. The U.S. government had begun plans to overthrow the Revolution late in the Eisenhower presidency. The CIA, in coordination with the Joint Chiefs of Staff in the U.S. Defense Department, recruited, trained, and equipped an army of exiles based in Guatemala to destroy the Revolution. To conceal its role as the author of the plan, the U.S. government employed instructors of Cuban origin, including former officers of Batista's armed forces.

On October 7, 1960, Cuba's Foreign Secretary, Raúl Roa, in an address at the United Nations, denounced the training of mercenary troops in Guatemala.

136   HOW THE WORKERS' PARLIAMENTS

But in 1961, under a new U.S. administration, the plan changed to an overt invasion of Cuba by an amphibious and airborne assault. The invasion would be supported by psychological war tactics and propaganda, weapons and explosives shipments to the island, and infiltration by U.S. agents.

Radio Swan was created to broadcast propaganda against the Cuban Revolution; other Miami-based efforts had the same mission. The radio stations broadcast false reports about a new Cuban law that purportedly would allow the revolutionary government to take children from five to eighteen years of age from their parents and send them to work on farms or to the Soviet Union to be indoctrinated. It was even said that some of these children would return to Cuba as Russian canned meat! This propaganda served as the basis for subversive campaigns such as the "Peter Pan" operation.[104] In the United States, the press spread misinformation and attacked Cuba.

Early in the morning of April 15, 1961, simultaneous aerial attacks were launched against the air base at San Antonio de los Baños,[105] the Ciudad Libertad landing strip,[106] and the Santiago de Cuba airport. Seven people died in those attacks, and more than fifty were wounded. The eight bomber planes used for the assaults bore the insignias of the Cuban Air Force. Five planes returned to the base in Nicaragua from which they had departed; one was brought down; and the other two made emergency landings in Cayo Hueso and Gran Caimán.

At an April 16, 1961, event honoring the victims of the attack, Fidel Castro denounced the details of the intervention and declared the socialist character of the Cuban Revolution. The next day the counterrevolutionary forces invaded Playa Larga, and, a few minutes later, Playa Girón (Bay of Pigs). They were soundly defeated. On April 23, the Cuban government presented evidence of the U.S. role in financing, preparing, and executing the armed aggression.

NEW PATHS

The first years of the revolutionary government brought major changes to Cuba. In September 1960, Cuba informed the United Nations

SAVED THE CUBAN REVOLUTION 137

General Assembly that it would undertake a massive adult literacy campaign. The campaign mobilized more than 2,000 literacy instructors, including schoolteachers, students, and workers. When the campaign ended on December 22, 707,212 illiterate Cubans had learned to read and write. Centuries of ignorance were left behind. The army of literacy teachers shared daily life with the peasants and the humblest families in what was truly an epic endeavor.

Cuba's transformation included its economy. The old landowning structure was eliminated, and land was turned over to tens of thousands of peasants, tenant farmers, and squatters.[107] The Revolution tackled unemployment and prioritized public health and education. The government built hospitals and polyclinics and brought medical services to remote rural zones. Under a new national system, primary education was made obligatory and new schools were opened. An extensive scholarship program put intermediate and higher education within the reach of the entire population. The government also encouraged the widespread diffusion of cultural activity—literature, visual arts, music, and film.

THE WAR AGAINST THE BANDITS

After the triumph of the Revolution, counterrevolutionary forces— former members of Batista's army and the dictatorship's repressive and paramilitary structures—took to the countryside where they staged a few isolated uprisings. They failed, thanks to the Rebel Army and *Milicias Nacionales Revolucionarias* (Revolutionary National Militias/ MNR). The U.S. government, despite its initial failures, fomented other attempts. Airplanes, flying at night and at low altitudes, parachuted wooden crates containing weapons, ammunition, explosives, means of communication, clothes, provisions, and medicines. These operations generally were coordinated with counterrevolutionary ringleaders through CIA agents inside the country.

Those bands and their leaders not only lacked ethical and patriotic values: they also had little social support. They were moved by personal interests, ambition, and deep hatred. They destroyed houses, schools,

138   HOW THE WORKERS' PARLIAMENTS

rural stores, and sugarcane plantations. and attacked mass transport. Peasants and farm workers were killed. The counterrevolutionaries plundered and sowed terror among the rural population to intimidate them into cooperating as they awaited a U.S. military intervention.

In July 1962, the revolutionary government initiated the War Against the Bandits. Squads, companies, and battalions were constituted, supplemented by thousands of militia members from various provinces. By the time the war ended in 1965, 549 members of the Cuban Revolutionary Armed Forces had been killed. (The death toll of the counterrevolutionaries and others, such as civilians and pro-government militias, is unknown.) Suppressing the rebellion cost Cuba approximately one billion pesos, during difficult years for the national economy.[108]

THE UNITED STATES TRIES TO ISOLATE CUBA

While Cuba was undergoing profound transformation in many spheres, the United States sought to isolate it internationally. The U.S. government pushed for Cuba's expulsion from the Organization of American States (OAS)—which Cuba had helped found in 1947–48. From 1962, when President John F. Kennedy secured enough votes to expel Cuba, to 2009, Cuba was suspended from the organization. (Cuba's membership was restored in June 2009, but it refused to rejoin the organization.)

An OAS conference held in San José, Costa Rica, in August 1960, had approved a declaration that created a legal justification for U.S. aggression against Cuba. In response to the so-called San José Declaration, more than a million Cubans gathered in Havana's Revolution Square to voice their approval of the First Havana Declaration, which upheld the self-determination, sovereignty, and dignity of Latin America while denouncing U.S. imperialism, which had impinged on the region for more than a century, since the declaration of the Monroe Doctrine.[109]

In January 1962, the OAS approved four resolutions against Cuba. Latin American governments, with the exception of Mexico, broke off diplomatic relations with the revolutionary government. This led to the Second Declaration of Havana, approved by acclamation in the General Assembly of the people, gathered, once again, in Revolution Square, on February 4, 1962. The Cuban people reasserted their intention to keep on resisting and to build socialism, despite all the difficulties and pressures.

THE MONGOOSE PLAN

After the defeat of U.S. aggression at Playa Girón, President John F. Kennedy approved the Mongoose Plan in November 1962. This new covert action plan included sabotage, psychological warfare, spying, and the fomenting of counterrevolution inside Cuba. The plan, executed by the CIA, used airplanes and high-speed motorboats to attack economic targets, towns, and cities. Vessels of countries that traded with Cuba and Cuban fishing vessels were attacked. Under Mongoose, there were more than 5,000 acts of sabotage and terrorism, including plans to assassinate Fidel Castro and other Cuban leaders. The United States set up clandestine networks, infiltrating agents into Cuba, accompanied by propaganda campaigns and other counterrevolutionary activities inside the country. The CIA even established links with the Mafia to carry out its campaign. Direct military aggression also was considered, under a contrived *casus belli* by which the United States would justify its actions before international public opinion. Given the possibility of direct military aggression against Cuba, the Cuban government bolstered the country's armed forces and the Revolutionary National Militias.

THE OCTOBER CRISIS

In 1962, a great threat hovered over the island. Cuba had requested that the USSR increase its arms shipments for the defensive military reinforcement and modernization of the FAR (Revolutionary Armed Forces). In an interview with the Spanish journalist Ignacio Ramonet, Fidel Castro disclosed that the Soviets had told Cuba about the existence of such danger, and they sent a delegation to speak with the Cuban leadership.[110] He offered details of that conversation and explained why Cuba decided to accept the installation of missiles on its territory. He defended the decision on the grounds that Cuba faced the actual danger of a U.S. invasion.

The Commander in Chief also explained how events had developed since U.S. spy planes detected and photographed the missile facilities. He cited the increased reconnaissance flights over the island, President Kennedy's decision to establish a naval blockade, and his October 22 address demanding the removal of the missiles and the destruction of the missile sites. October 27 was the day of maximum tension, when Soviet rockets in Oriente province brought down a U-2 spy plane.

Fidel criticized the Soviet Union for failing to defend Cuba and its decision to request Soviet support against U.S. aggression. On October 25, the USSR's United Nations ambassador instead denied the authenticity of the evidence that the United States presented. Cuba also was excluded from discussions between the U.S. and Soviet governments regarding the missiles. Fidel insisted that Cuba's position, comprising five demands, be included in all negotiations. A true non-aggression pact would abolish the naval blockade; revoke the economic blockade and the U.S. commercial and economic pressures; cease subversive activities, including the delivery of weapons and explosives by air or sea; prohibit invasions by mercenary forces organized by the United States; cease the infiltration of spies and saboteurs into Cuba and actions initiated from the United States and some of its allies; end attacks from bases in the United States and Puerto Rico; cease all violations of the Cuban air and naval space by U.S. airplanes and warships; and mandate U.S. withdrawal from the naval base at Guantánamo. Cuba also refused to permit inspections of its territory.

The world was on the verge of a thermonuclear war as a consequence of the U.S. aggression against Cuba. Twenty years after these events, when documents related to the crisis were declassified and published by the United States, the full details of what the Kennedy administration had planned for Cuba became known.

Che Guevara, in a letter to Fidel, wrote: "I felt, by your side, the pride

SAVED THE CUBAN REVOLUTION   141

of belonging to our people in the bright and sad days of the Caribbean crisis.... I take pride in having followed you without hesitation, having identified with your way of thinking, seeing and appreciating the dangers and the principles."[111]

CUBA BUILT; THE UNITED STATES ATTACKED

For years, the United States carried out terrorist attacks against Cuban diplomats and other Cubans outside the country. On October 6, 1976, a Cuban flight headed from Barbados to Havana was blown up, killing seventy-three people, including twenty-four members of Cuba's fencing team. The eleven Guyanese and five Koreans on board also died.

The United States also waged biological warfare against Cuba. In 1971, African swine fever was introduced into the island, which required the mass slaughter of pigs and a prolonged halt in hog breeding. There were recurrences of African swine fever in 1979 and 1980. In 1978, a fungal pathogen known as orange rust destroyed cultivation of the high-yield Barbados 4362 sugarcane variety. In 1979, blue mold, an airborne fungus, destroyed two successive tobacco harvests. In 1981, hemorrhagic dengue fever caused the death of 158 Cubans, including 61 children. Pathogens were introduced into beans, potatoes, peppers, bananas, and rice.

Fabián Escalante, a Major General who wrote several books about U.S. intelligence services, revealed in December 2016 that Cuban state security entities had discovered and dismantled 634 U.S. plots.

Beginning in January 1959, the United States also encouraged migration as a way to undermine the Revolution. The United States offered its protection and asylum to murderers, torturers, embezzlers, and thieves of the Batista dictatorship. Washington rejected the extradition requests for notorious criminals. The U.S. government particularly promoted an exodus of professionals and qualified personnel. In 1966, the U.S. Congress approved the Cuban Adjustment Act, which offered Cubans privileges not granted to citizens of any other country, including an expedited path to permanent residency and U.S. citizenship.

142   HOW THE WORKERS' PARLIAMENTS

In the context of U.S. aggression and threats, Cuba strengthened its links with the Socialist Bloc and Third World nations. Cuba joined the Non-Aligned Nations movement founded in Yugoslavia in 1961. The revolutionary government's policy was to actively support national liberation movements.

On October 3, 1965, the Communist Party of Cuba was founded. The party that leads Cuba did not emerge from fragmentation or division but from the unity of all revolutionary forces. It was a successor of the United Party of the Cuban Socialist Revolution, which comprised the July 26 Movement and the Popular Socialist Party.

Between December 17 and 22, 1975, the party's First Congress addressed the reorganization of the economy, the strengthening of mass organizations, the party's work, and the state's central administration. A new political-administrative division was established. Fourteen provinces were designated, 169 municipalities, and one municipality with special character (Isla de Pinos), which in 1978 was renamed Isla de la Juventud (Isle of Youth). It was the beginning of a new phase in the country's economic, political, and social life.

TRANSFORMATIONS OF CUBAN ECONOMY AND SOCIETY

The process of transformation of Cuba's economy and society reached its maximum expression in the Gross Domestic Product (GDP) from 1980 to 1985. Data published in 2009 show that between 1961 and 1965 the GDP increased at an annual rate of 1.9 percent; from 1966 to 1970, 3.9 percent; from 1971 to 1975, an annual average rate of 7 percent; from1976 to 1980, 4 percent. [112]

Cuba set a goal of 10 million tons of sugar in 1970, a huge challenge, given the country's organizational, technical, and material conditions. When the goal was not reached, the government reassessed its policy, including technology issues, insufficient labor force, economic management, and obsolete methods. Despite these problems, 8,537,600 tons of sugar were produced, the greatest harvest in Cuban history.

In 1972, Cuba joined the Council for Mutual Economic Assistance (COMECON), an economic organization founded in 1949 under the

SAVED THE CUBAN REVOLUTION 143

leadership of the Soviet Union that comprised the Eastern Bloc and other socialist states.

From 1973 to 1975, Cuba's sugar production made a qualitative leap. Sugar mills were reconstructed; the skills of workers and technicians were enhanced; the mechanization of cane cutting was improved. Agriculture expanded to rice and citrus fruits. Pork, beef, and poultry production grew. Dams and reservoirs were constructed. Parts of the country were reforested. From the early to mid-1970s, Cuba established a national mercantile fleet and new fishing fleets, and built shipyards and industrial plants. Mining, production of oil and petroleum derivatives, steel production, and electric power generation gradually increased. Roads were built.

Little by little, Cuba made significant advances in the quality of life of its people: personal consumption, salaries, electrification, social security, and labor policy, increased participation by women in the workforce, and job creation. Cuba also made major strides in public health, education, culture, sports, science, and technology.

Foreign trade also was reorganized. When the Revolution triumphed, 70 percent of Cuba's trade was conducted with the United States. The imposition of the U.S. economic blockade necessitated new sources for raw materials, equipment, medicines, and food, and for markets for Cuban products. Cuba established new and generally favorable trade relationships, but the trading partners' geographic distance from Cuba increased shipping and other costs.

From 1980 to 1985, industry, agriculture, and transportation improved. Labor productivity rose, while the costs of production and energy decreased. Sugar production grew, with modernized and larger production plants and mechanized harvesting. Hydraulic works, railways, roads, and highways were constructed. In public health, hospitals and other facilities were remodeled and enlarged.

All these advances notwithstanding, significant problems remained. They included an unstable workforce, losses in construction, and less than optimal use of agricultural technology and equipment. Salary incentives—bonuses and other rewards—often did not yield their anticipated results in improved performance of entities. The economic

144 HOW THE WORKERS' PARLIAMENTS

management and planning system based on the experience of other countries proved unsuitable to Cuba's specific conditions.

In December 1986, coinciding with the thirtieth anniversary of the *Granma*'s disembarking, Fidel Castro stated that if the errors and the negative tendencies were not corrected, the program that the Communist Party approved in its Congress earlier that year could not be implemented.

RECTIFYING ERRORS

The process of rectification of errors and negative tendencies began. Along with the search for solutions to economic problems, ideological and social concerns, Cuba's youth and the peasantry were scrutinized. The relationship between cooperative farms and state entities also was analyzed.

Fidel insisted that the construction of socialism was not a mechanical process but a political, revolutionary task. The process he was calling for had to be conducted in the midst of a shortage of foreign currency, which had fallen from 1.2 billion dollars to 600 million. There were other pressing concerns: drought had affected sugar production, and Cuban oil export prices fell. Meanwhile, the U.S. economic blockade continued to limit economic growth. All these factors contributed to a 40 percent decline in income.

Cuba, however, was determined to face these challenges without sacrificing its economic or social future. But its model of socialism would have to be rectified. From 1985 to 1990, Cuba entered a new phase in which it had to defend the Revolution's very existence. The process of correcting ideological, political, and economic problems paid off. In just two years, in Havana alone, 111 kindergartens and twenty-four special education schools were built, as well as twenty polyclinics and 1,600 surgeries staffed by family doctors and nurses. More than 18,000 houses were built by "micro brigades," a form of workplace organization in which workers left their regular jobs, often for years, to build homes.[113]

The capacity of the Cuban people to face up to such great

SAVED THE CUBAN REVOLUTION   145

difficulties, the sudden loss of means and resources that had sustained the development of the country up to that point, can only be explained by their history of resistance since the triumph of January 1, 1959. The Revolution consolidated the aspirations of the great majority of Cubans. Their sense of ownership of the gains it made fostered perseverance and a tenacity that enabled them to make the sacrifices entailed by the Special Period.

THE REVOLUTION'S SOCIAL INITIATIVES

The Cuban Revolution's social initiatives focused on education, public health, culture, science, and sports.

After the completion of the adult literacy campaign, Cubans who had become literate were able to continue their studies. In fact, the Revolution made free education available at all levels. The State increased education spending by large increments. More children than ever, from ages six to twelve and thirteen to sixteen, were in school. A national scholarship program was established. Thousands of schools were created, as were training institutes for teachers. The University Reform Law made higher education available to workers and their children while expanding degree programs. The Revolution turned education into a pillar of Cuba's present and future.

Let's compare these results with pre-Revolution education data. Nearly one-quarter of Cuba's population, some one million people, did not know how to read or write. There were 9,000 unemployed teachers; 50 percent of school-age children in the countryside did not attend school, which contributed to high rates of adult illiteracy.

Public health was another priority of the Revolution. Before the Revolution, the infant mortality rate was sixty of every 1,000 live births; today, it is less than five. Life expectancy was fifty-five years; today, it is nearly eighty. In the 1950s, there were only a little more than 6,000 physicians, most of them in Havana. Today, there are 74,000, distributed nationwide. These data are crucial to understanding how profoundly the Revolution transformed this critical sphere.

Public health services, including vaccination, maternal-child care,

146   HOW THE WORKERS' PARLIAMENTS

and preventive medicine, were offered free of charge. Medical services in rural areas were substantially expanded, and the number of hospitals, medical centers, blood banks, polyclinics, stomatology clinics, maternal homes, laboratories, and specialized research centers increased. Given the loss of thousands of doctors who fled the country, encouraged by the U.S. government, the revolutionary government created many medical and nursing schools to train a new corps of health care providers.

From its earliest years, the revolutionary government laid the foundation of a public health system that has won international acclaim—the World Health Organization (WHO) has acknowledged Cuba's remarkable accomplishments in protecting the health of its people. Not only that, Cuba has altruistically provided medical and health services to people in need worldwide. When COVID-19 struck, Cuba sent health care teams to nearly forty countries to help them cope with the pandemic.[114]

In culture, the Revolution sought to recuperate Cuba's traditions and reassert its national identity. Great literature was published and reading was promoted. The government established publishing houses, bookshops, museums, theaters, art galleries, and schools. In 1959, it founded the Cuban Institute of Cinematographic Art and Industry and the Casa de las Américas (House of the Americas). The cinema institute supported a new film industry, whose works were internationally acclaimed. The Casa de las Americas promotes literature, music, visual and plastic arts, theater, and cultural and social science research about Latin America and the Caribbean.

Fidel Castro declared the principles of Cuban cultural policy in a 1961 speech that has come to be known as *"Palabras a los intelectuales"* (Words to the Intellectuals). That year also saw the founding of the *Unión Nacional de Escritores y Artistas de Cuba* (National Union of Writers and Artists of Cuba). In 1976, the Ministry of Culture was established under Armando Hart Dávalos. New institutions emerged to research, preserve, and maintain Cuba's cultural patrimony.

In a January 15, 1960, speech, Fidel Castro said, "The future of our homeland necessarily has to be a future of science." This expressed priority led to the creation of many new scientific research centers.

In the 1980s, Cuba accelerated its biotechnology program, creating research projects and building an infrastructure. During the 1990s, the government created research centers where scientists from various disciplines made innovations in biomedical, information, and communications technologies. The first center, established in Havana in 1991, developed health and nutrition biotechnologies to benefit Cubans and for export.

Cuba's scientific development originated in the integration of the sciences, in mutual support, the exchange of experiences and knowledge, and the work performed in the centers set up throughout the country.

The Revolution also prioritized sports as a way to promote health and raise the quality of life. Sports facilities were constructed and physical education was included in the curricula of all schools, from kindergarten to university. The government established a system to train and develop the athletes and physical education instructors of the future. In 1961, the National Institute of Sports, Physical Education, and Recreation was founded, followed later by the National Sports Industry and the Institute of Sports Medicine. Sports events were organized in schools to identify new talents and then link them to specialized centers, where their skills would be further developed.

THE CUBAN REVOLUTION'S FOREIGN POLICY

Ever since the its earliest years, the Cuban Revolution based its foreign policy on alliances with parties, governments, and peoples of the Union of Soviet Socialist Republics and the socialist nations, and on support for the national liberation movements in the Third World. Cuba established relations of mutual respect with nations that acknowledged the island's sovereignty and independence.

Cuba demonstrated solidarity to national liberation movements in the Third World. This included scholarships for professionals and technicians of developing nations and the assignment of Cuban professionals

148 HOW THE WORKERS' PARLIAMENTS

and technicians, especially in public health, to assist countries experiencing natural disasters. The first such brigade was sent to Algeria in 1963, not long after that nation obtained its independence. Despite the loss of physicians in the early years of the Revolution, Cuba did not hesitate to share its doctors with other nations.

The support offered Africa, a continent with deep historical and cultural ties to the Antilles, stands out. When the Revolution triumphed in 1959, several African countries still were colonies. South Africa's black and mxed-race people were oppressed by the apartheid system.[115] Cuba supported Algerian patriots in their struggle against French colonialism at the expense of its political and economic relations with France, then still an important power; the shipment of weapons and combatants to defend Algeria from Moroccan aggression.[116] The tanks sent to Syria between 1973 and 1975 stood guard in the Golan Heights, when that Syrian territory was seized by Israel.[117] Aid to Patrice Lumumba, the Congolese leader assassinated in 1961 by forces linked to the United States and the former colonial power Belgium, after the country gained its independence.[118] Four years later, in 1965, Cuban blood was shed in the western zone of Tanganyika Lake,[119] where Che, with more than one hundred Cuban instructors, supported the Congolese rebels who fought mercenaries serving the Congolese dictator Mobuto Sese Seko.[120] Cuban instructors trained and supported the combatants of the African Party for the Independence of Guinea and Cape Verde, which under the command of Amílcar Cabral, fought for the independence of these Portuguese colonies.[121]

Cuba expressed solidarity with the Vietnamese during the war waged against their country by the United States. Cuban and Latin American blood was shed in Bolivia, where Che Guevara was killed in 1967 under instructions of U.S. agents. In 1981, Cuban construction workers were helping to build an international airport on the Caribbean island of Grenada when the United States invaded under false pretexts. In Nicaragua, Cuban military instructors trained soldiers who were defending the Sandinista revolution in the war of subversion that was organized and armed by the United States.

SAVED THE CUBAN REVOLUTION

Cuban involvement in Angola was another noteworthy example of Cuban internationalism. In 1974, a military coup overthrew Portugal's authoritarian government, leading to the independence of Portuguese colonies. On January 31, 1975, a transition government was formed in Angola, with authority distributed among the Portuguese colonial administration, the Movement for the Liberation of Angola (MPLA), the National Front of Angola (FNLA) led by Holden Roberto, and the National Union for the Total Independence of Angola (UNITA), led by Jonas Savimbi.

In November of 1975, Cuba, at the request of MPLA, sent 500 instructors to train its combatants. When South Africa invaded Angola to crush the MPLA and drive out the Cuban soldiers, Cuba sent more forces to repel the apartheid state's aggression. This was the beginning of Operation Carlota (named for the enslaved Black rebel killed in 1843).

With a force comprising thousands of troops, the South Africans attacked Luanda, the capital. The Cubans and the Angolans repelled the first attack. South Africa attacked again, with superior forces, on November 10, one day before independence was to be proclaimed. Once again, the MPLA and Cuban fighters prevailed, and on November 11, President Agostinho Neto proclaimed the birth of the independent Popular Republic of Angola. After more than fifteen years, in May 1991, the last Cuban troops remaining in Angola returned to Cuba.

In 1962, Nelson Mandela, the leader of the African National Congress, the leading anti-apartheid force in South Africa, was arrested and sentenced to five years in prison. Two years later, the sentence was extended to life imprisonment. After almost twenty-eight years in prison, he was released in 1990 because of local and international pressure. He received numerous international honors, including, in 1993, the Nobel Peace Prize. When he visited Cuba in 1991, on the anniversary of the July 26, 1953, assault on the Moncada fortress, he said, "The Cuban people occupies a special place in the heart of the peoples of Africa. The Cuban internationalists made a contribution to Independence, freedom and justice in Africa without parallel for the principles and the unselfishness that characterize them."

EPILOGUE

Writing this book was not simply an exercise in revisiting past events or in nostalgia. My intention was to reflect on history in order to contribute to a fuller understanding of the present. To analyze the past, the good and the bad in our Cuban history, with an eye to the future, I have related personal and collective experiences of many comrades over many years. We learned from those who suffered and fought before us. We studied the past to prepare us for the new challenges we faced. We hope that what we have learned and done will prove useful to those rising up today against injustice and oppression.

Fidel and Raúl Castro, and those Cubans who made up what we call the "centenary generation"—those who rose up on the one-hundredth anniversary of Jose Martí's birth in 1953—started as outstanding students and became exemplary teachers. That's why those young men and women embarked on a new assault on the heavens; they felt themselves to be heirs of the best of the *mambí* traditions and champions of Martí's legacy.

As I write these final lines, Cuba keeps moving forward on its revolutionary path. Cubans have learned from experience that building socialism entails a prolonged, heterogeneous, complex, and contradictory process of profound political, economic, and social transformation. Socialist consolidation and progress require political and ideological unity and the active participation of the people, under sound leadership.

The revolutionary government initiated a radical transformation of property relations. Landowning was eliminated and the means of production were substantially nationalized. State ownership was decisive in Cuba's socioeconomic transformation, putting an end to the neocolonial capitalist phase of our history and initiating the transition toward a society whose socialist character was proclaimed by Fidel on April 16, 1961.

As Cuba built socialism, it endured aggression that caused enormous human and material losses. The revolutionary government was forced to allocate substantial resources to national defense and security,

SAVED THE CUBAN REVOLUTION 151

despite shortages and to the detriment of the country's development. Successive U.S. administrations have maintained a hostile policy toward Cuba, through terrorism and subversion, and a prolonged economic, financial, and commercial blockade that, for more than half a century, has prevented Cuba from gaining access to sources of finance, equipment, services, and products.

However, Cuba, despite its errors and inefficiencies, has made remarkable progress—political, social, cultural, scientific and technical, and economic.

After the disintegration of the Soviet Union and the European Socialist Bloc, Cuba suffered from the loss of economic and commercial relations with those powers. The scientific and technical collaborations also ended. At the same time, neoliberal economics and politics became dominant, and the United States asserted its hegemonic dominance. It intensified its blockade, political and ideological subversion, and terrorism.

At the beginning of the 1990s, Cuba entered a new, difficult phase: the Special Period in peacetime. The economy deteriorated, as did the quality of life. Cuba was forced to adapt its economy to the new circumstances while still maintaining the Revolution's ideals and major achievements.

The Cuban leadership could not adopt extraordinary measures without the involvement and approval of the Cuban people. Hence the creation of the forums that Fidel called workers' parliaments. In them, more than three million workers, men and women—as well as youth and students, peasants and members of agricultural cooperatives—engaged in intense and ultimately fruitful debates about how the country should respond to the challenges of the Special Period.

In the first part of this book, I described how the workers' parliaments were conceived, organized, and developed. The measures they adopted, with majoritarian support, preserved as much as possible public health, education, jobs and salaries, pensions and benefits. Some free services were eliminated, and the prices of some goods and services rose.

During the Special Period, Cuba permitted foreign investment and freelance work in certain areas. It established the Basic Units of Cooperative Production and agricultural markets, and granted lands in usufruct to encourage agricultural production.

This period also saw the reorganization of the state's central administration. Many government entities were resized to adjust their functions and reduce excess staff.

In monetary and fiscal exchange, holding and circulating foreign currency was legalized and remittances from abroad were permitted. Cuba also set two types of exchange rates—one mainly for relations among state-owned entities, the other for the population and non-state institutions.

In 1994, the economy began its gradual recovery, albeit under the circumstances imposed by the blockade, the uncertain international economy, and internal difficulties and deficiencies. I have not addressed the last of those critical circumstances until now. However, they must be acknowledged. We have not advanced at an optimal pace, nor have we solved the structural problems inherent to an underdeveloped economy.

The economic problems include a disconnect between work performed and its remuneration; needs and the lack of foreign currency available to meet them; insufficient supply of goods and services to satisfy growing demand; and imbalances between imports and exports.

Cuban agriculture has been hindered by low productivity and inefficiency. Industry has suffered from technological obsolescence, excessive dependence on non-renewable sources, and limited productive chains, as well as environmental risks and damages. Production, services, and investment have been poorly organized and managed.

Negative phenomena have proliferated in parts of Cuban society— behavior that flouts our principles and values, a reluctance to work more efficiently, manifestations of individualism, bureaucracy, corruption, and indiscipline.

In the international field, the structural crisis of the world capitalist system persists. Concentrated wealth, extreme inequality, and high poverty levels are exacerbated by social and ecological crises, wars, and massive migrations.

SAVED THE CUBAN REVOLUTION 153

At the same time, advances in science, technology, communications, computerization, industry, food production, transport, public health, and education offer significant opportunities to develop socialism. A diverse and committed civil society has been and will continue to be indispensable to that task in Cuba.

We Cubans will keep striving to achieve a socialist society, prosperous and sustainable, based on a profound revolutionary conscience and sense of duty, by working with efficiency and efficacy, making the best, most rational use of our human and material resources. If this book, whatever its shortcomings and limitations, gives readers a better sense of what the Cuban Revolution has achieved and aims to achieve in the future, I will be satisfied.

Onward to victory, always. We shall overcome.

Appendix

Bibliography

Notes

APPENDIX A

TOPIC 1: ECONOMIC EFFICIENCY	FREQ.	%
• Increase or stimulate production.	19,953	45
• Combat economic offenses.	13,158	30
• Improve the quality of production.	11,104	25
Increase and Stimulate Production		Mun.*
• Increase production and services as the main way to reorganize finances efficiently, with a stable provision to the public.	7,520	155
• Enterprises must increase production of items demanded by the public.	3,956	94
• Allocate idle lands to workers, peasants, and pensioners while preserving state ownership; levy taxes.	2,260	89
• Investigate mechanisms that link workers and self-supply activities to achieve greater productivity.	2,086	26
• Each enterprise should have its own self-supply area for workers' canteens and sell, if possible, products to the employees.	1,868	86
• Work to make enterprises profitable, seeking alternative formulas wherever possible.	1,320	86
• Non-profitable enterprises should not be subsidized.	1,241	85
Combat Economic Offenses		
• Strengthen control of financial and material resources, shortfalls and and losses; implement severe sanctions for misappropriation of state goods.	6,583	134
• Control the black-market sale of medications.	2,525	57
• Supervise, through a group of inspectors, everything related to prices.	2,437	21
• Increase administrative control of production and services.	1,613	55
Monitor Quality of Production and Personnel Selection.		
Conservation of Resources		
• Achieve more rational use of material resources, electric-power generators, and raw materials.	6,619	85
• Improve the quality of production and services through greater oversight, preventing the waste of resources.	1,795	109
• Establish prices of products and services based on quality.	1,570	37
• Rigorously select the personnel to work in the tourist sector.	170	26
• Analyze the possibility that part of the foreign currency derived from the results obtained from production stays in the workplace to cover their needs.	14	2
• Demand that administrators distribute merchandise at the municipal level, to prevent delays in the delivery of the same to the population.	7	4
• Allow dairy farms autonomy in sales to the public.	1	1

*Municipalities

APPENDIX 157

TOPIC 2: WORKFORCE AND DISCIPLINE	FREQ.	%
• Labor legislation to combat offenses.	11,893	34
• Workers' services.	10,561	30
• Rational reorganization of the workforce.	6,206	18
• Control of freelance workers.	6,616	18
Labor Legislation and its Fulfilment		
• Better use of the workday.	3,537	132
• Verification of medical certificates.	1,941	89
• Workplace management must be tough on offenders and fulfill labor legislation.	1,938	122
• More rigorous Ministry of Public Health oversight of the issuance of medical certificate.	1,817	84
• Take into account the skills, age, and other factors with respect to redundant personnel.	1,447	2
• Mandatory retirement of the workers when they reach retirement age.	973	36
• Revise labor legislation so that it is less paternalistic and more in accordance with reality.	569	82
Incentives Based on Work Performance		
• Improve worker performance in all entities and enterprises; reward those who deserve it, materially and morally.	8,911	153
• Reorganization of finances, paying each worker according to his/her work performance.	1,650	93
• Incentivize workers by means of specialized shops with national and international products.	605	40
Reorganization of Personnel in State Enterprises		
• Relocate redundant personnel to prioritized work.	2,670	120
• Readjust the staff of workplaces, whenever possible, to obtain greater productivity and lower salary costs. Relocate personnel to agriculture and similar areas.	2,438	76
• Reduce the staff of administrative and management bureaucracies.	1,170	79
• Decentralize state hiring and the approval of staff.	5	3
Control of Freelance Workers		
• Establish a state fee structure for freelance work.	2,675	95
• Take income into account in levying taxes.	2,092	91
• Revise the granting of licenses; no licenses should be granted to *macetas*.	1,520	48
• Analyze the use of raw materials production.	1,318	65
• Establish a system to regulate the fees applied to freelance workers.	1,103	47
• Make a thorough analysis of how and to whom licenses are granted.	964	29
• Form trade unions of freelance workers.	550	30

TOPIC 3: PROPOSALS FOR BUDGETARY BALANCE AND THE REORGANIZATION OF DOMESTIC FINANCES	FREQ.	%
• Eliminate subsidies.	39,949	36
• Combat financial offenses.	19,784	18
• Maintain subsidies.	16,712	15
• Establish more effective price policies.	13,459	12
• Change currency.	10,834	10
• Implement a tax policy.	9,966	9
Elimination of Non-Fundamental Subsidies		
• Charge for electivve surgeries and other similar services.	11,507	137
• Charge for recreational activities.	8,863	164
• Charge for cultural activities.	6,000	162
• Charge for medical assistance in cases of traffic accidents and physical aggression.	3,201	107
• Charge for the study material and school uniforms.	1,602	120
• Charge for water service at a reasonable price.	1,145	90
• Charge for higher, postgraduate, language, and other non-basic studies.	687	68
• Charge for university studies for those who unjustifiably drop out or do not utilize those skills after graduation.	620	66
Penal Code		
• Confiscate money and assets of those who have enriched themselves illicitly.	14,904	159
• Abolish *macetas*.	3,190	45
• Revise the penal code.	1,690	89
• Confiscate goods, motorcycles, cars, and other similar items sold by the state that are not currently the property of their original owner.	632	41
• Revise or increase the fines system.	138	12
• Impose more severe sanctions for citizens who commit offenses.	498	16
Maintaining Subsidies of the Revolution		
• No charges for any public health or education services considered an achievement of the Revolution.	5,217	134
• Maintain prices of essential items.	3,439	113
• Preserve free education services.	3,318	88
• No charge for sports activities.	2,188	85
• No increase in public transportation.	1,396	51
• Take workers' salaries into account when analyzing the price increase of transportation services.	1,154	40
• Subsidize low-income families.	932	78
Establish More Effective Price Policies		
• Deregulate and moderately increase the prices of cigarettes and cigars.	5,035	130
• Deregulate and increase the price of alcoholic drinks.	1,409	71
• Normalize the deregulated sale of cigars.	1,323	24

APPENDIX

TOPIC 3: PROPOSALS FOR BUDGETARY BALANCE AND THE REORGANIZATION OF DOMESTIC FINANCES	FREQ.	%
Establish More Effective Price Policies (cont'd)		
• Maintain the established quota of cigarettes; eliminate the additional quota; establish stable prices for the deregulated sale of cigarettes.	1,106	56
• Distribute rum per family unit at a reasonable price.	1,036	33
• Analyze the prices charged at workers' cafeterias.	427	22
• Implement a national lottery to raise state revenue (games of chance, cockfighting, etc.).	77	21
Currency		
• Carry out a change of currency at a national level to collect the money supply.	6,472	158
• No change in currency, because the country is not in economic condition to do so.	3,043	109
	1,319	52
• Changing currency will not solve the country's financial problems.	4,955	99
Tax Policy		
• No taxes on salary.	2,917	87
• Create peasant free markets, applying direct taxes and state prices.		
• Levy taxes on peasants based on their income.	800	55

Bibliography

Almeida Bosque, Juan, *The Sierra Maestra and Beyond* (Havana: Editora Política, 1995).

Alonso, Guillermo, and Enrique Vignier, *Political and Administrative Corruption in Cuba, 1944–1952* (Havana: Social Sciences Publishing House, 1973).

Álvarez Tabío, Pedro, *The Conquest of Hope, Ernesto Che Guevara and Raúl Castro Ruz Campaign Newspapers* (Havana: Ediciones Verde Olivo, 2005).

Barnet, Miguel, *Biography of a Maroon* (Havana: Editorial Academia, 1986).

Blanco Castiñeira, Katiuska, *All the Time of the Cedars* (Havana: Casa Editorial Abril, 2003).

_____, *Fidel Castro Ruz, Time warrior,* vols. 1 and 2 (Havana: Casa Editora Abril, 2011).

Betto, Frei, *Fidel and Religion* (Havana: Office of Publications of the Council of State, 1985).

Bravo, Estela Y Gómez Cortés, and Olga Rosa, *Operation Peter Pan: Closing the Circle in Cuba* (Havana: Editorial Casa de las Américas, 2013).

Cantón Navarro, José, *Cuba, el desafío del yugo y la estrella* (Havana: Editorial SI-MAR S.A., 1996).

Cantón Navarro and José Y Silva León, Arnaldo, *History of Cuba 1959–1999* (Havana: Editorial Pueblo y Educación, 2009).

Castro Ruz, Fidel, *History Will Absolve Me,* Preface, Introduction, and Notes by Pedro Álvarez Tabío and Guillermo Alonso (Havana: Office of Publications of the Council of State, 1995).

_____. *The Strategic Counteroffensive* (Havana: Editorial Office of the Council of State Publications, 2010).

BIBLIOGRPAHY

SPEECHES

Fourth Congress of the FELAP, July 1985. Twentieth anniversary of the landing of the *Granma,* February 26, 1986.

Closing of the deferred session of the Third Congress of the Communist Party of Cuba, December 2, 1986.

Thirty-fifth anniversary of the assault on the Moncada fortress, 1988.

Commemoration of the thirtieth anniversary of the triumph of the Revolution, January 1, 1989.

Visit of Mikhail S. Gorbachev to Cuba, April 4, 1989.

Thirty-sixth anniversary of the assault on the Moncada fortress, July 26, 1989.

Closing of the Sixteenth CTC Congress, January 28, 1990.

Inauguration of the Fourth Congress of the Cuban Communist Party, October 10, 1991.

Closing of the Sixth National Forum on Spare Parts, Equipment and Advanced Technologies, December 16, 1991.

Fifth Congress of the National Union of Agricultural Workers, November 22, 1991.

Forty-third anniversary of the assault on the Moncada fortress, July 26, 1996.

Provincial Assembly of the Party of Havana City, November 23, 1996.

Fifth Congress of the Cuban Communist Party, October 10, 1997.

Angola Giron africano (Havana: Social Sciences Publishing House, 1976).

Victoria de las ideas, vols. 1–3 (Havana: Editora Política).

Con la razón histórica y la moral de Baraguá 1962 Crisis de Octubre (Havana: Editora Política, 1990).

Pagar tributo al imperio o pagar tributo a la patria (Havana: Editora Política, 1985).

United in a Single Cause, under a Single Flag (Havana: Editora Política, 1991).

Loyal To the Truth (Havana: Editora Política. 1992).

We Defend the Ideas and Values of the Country (Havana: Editora Política, 1992).

The Reason Is Ours, appearance on radio and television (Havana: Editora Política, 1994).

Times to Meditate and to Do (Havana: Editora Política, 1989).

El pensamiento y la conciencia pueden más que el terror y la muerte (Havana: Oficina de Publicaciones del Consejo de Estado, 2001).

Castro Ruz, Raúl, *Operation Carlota Is Over! Victory of Cuban Internationalism* (Havana: Editora Política, 1991).

Chomón, Faure, *The Assault on the Presidential Palace* (Havana: Social Sciences Publishing House, 1969).

Constitution of the Republic of Cuba (Havana, 1992).

Constitutions of Cuba, 1869–1940 (Havana: Editora Política, 1978).

Collazo, Enrique. *Cuba Intervenida* (incomplete).

162   BIBLIOGRPAHY

Demand of the Cuban People Against the United States Government for Damages Caused to Cuba, (Havana: Editora Política 2000).

Diario De Campaña Del Mayor Géximo Gómez, 1868–1899 (Havana: Centro Superior Tecnológico Ceiba del Agua, 1940).

Diez Acosta, Tomás, *La guerra encubierta contra Cuba* (Havana: Editora Política, 2002).

Speeches Speakers Central Act for May 1, 2003 (Havana: Editora Política, 2003).

Central Political Direction of the FAR, *History of Cuba* (Havana: Cuban Book Institute, 1971).

Central Documents of the Third and Fourth Party Congress: Appeals, Reports, Resolutions.

Analysis of the Scope and Content of the So-Called Helms-Burton Law (Havana: Editora Política, 1996).

Etcheverry Vázquez, Pedro Y Gutiérrez Oceguera, Santiago, *Banditry, Defeat of the CIA* (Havana: Editorial Capitán San Luis, 2008).

Etcheverry Vázquez, Pedro, *Banditry and Playa Girón* (Havana: Editorial Ocean Press-Editora Política, 2001).

Font, Fabián, *The CIA's Secret War* (Havana: Editorial Capitán San Luis, 1993).

Franklin, Jane, *Cuba-United States, Chronology of a History* (Havana: Social Sciences Publishing House, 2015).

Gálvez, William, *Camilo, Lord of the Vanguard* (Havana: Social Sciences Publishing House, 1979).

El sueño africano del Che (Havana: Editorial Casa de las Américas, 1997).

Gleyeses, Piero, Risquet Valdés, Jorge, and Ramírez De Estenoz, Fernando, *Cuba and Africa, common history of struggle and blood* (Havana: Social Sciences Publishing House, 2007).

_____, *Misiones en conflicto* (Havana: Social Sciences Publishing House, 2002).

_____, *The Cuban Epic: La misión del mundo de Fidel Castro (*Havana: Social Sciences Publishing House, 2009).

González Santamaría, Abel Enrique, *Fidel Castro and the United States, 90 Speeches, Interventions and Reflections* (compilation) (Havana: Editorial Capitán San Luis, 2017).

Hart Dávalos, Armando, *Change the rules of the game.* Interview by Luis Baez (Havana: Editorial Letras Cubanas, 1983).

International Conference José Martí, Universal Man (Havana: Centro de Estudios Martianos, April 1992).

The 1940 Constitution, digital version of *Juventud Rebelde*, October 9, 2010.

Ibarra, Jorge, *José Martí, leader, politician and ideologist* (Havana: Centro de Estudios Martianos, 2008).

Central Report to the Third and Fourth Congress of the Cuban Communist Party (Havana: Editora Política).

BIBLIOGRPAHY 163

Institute of History of Cuba, *History of Cuba* vol. 1 (Havana: Editora Política, 1994).

———, *La neocolonia, organización y crisis* (Havana: Editora Política, 1998).

Keeran, Roger, and Kenny, Thomas, *Tacit Socialism* (Havana: Social Science Publishing House, 2015).

Lamrani, Salim, *Fidel Castro, Cuba and the United States: Conversations with Ricardo Alarcón de Quesada* (Havana: Editorial José Martí, 2007).

50 truths about Fulgencio Batista in Cuba, Cubadebate digital publication, October 19, 2013.

The Republic: Dependence and Revolution (Havana: Book Institute, 1973).

Economic History of Cuba (Havana: Book Institute, 1967).

———, *José Martí: Thought and Action* (Havana: Editorial Centro de Estudios Martianos, 2012).

Leal Spengler, Eusebio, *Carlos Manuel de Céspedes, the lost newspaper* (Havana: Social Sciences Publishing House, 1994).

Leal Spengler, Eusebio, and Alarcón De Quesada, Ricardo, *Patria de humanidad y justicia, solemn session of the National Assembly of People's Power* (Havana: Editora Política, 1995).

Lee, Susana, Pagés, Raiza Y Oramas, Joaquín. *To rectify is to create* (Havana: Editora Política, 1989).

Marinello, Juan, *18 Martí's Essays* (Havana: Ediciones Unión, 1998).

Martí Pérez, José Julián, *La edad de oro (The Golden Age)* 5th ed. (Cuban Book Institute, Gente Nueva, 1999).

———, *Complete Works* vols. 1, 3, 4, 8, 10, 16, 19, 20 (Havana: Social Sciences Publishing House, 1975).

Martínez Pírez, Pedro, Interview with Dr. Eusebio Leal Spengler, "We Could Not Understand the Revolution Without the Republic," in *Temas* magazine, published in the *Boletín Por Cuba, de Cubarte* 41, May 26, 2017.

Memories of the Sixteenth CTC Congress (Havana: Social Sciences Publishing House, 1991).

Mencía, Mario. *The Fertile Prison* (Havana: Editora Política, 1980).

Miná, Gianni, *A meeting with Fidel* (Havana: Office of Publications of the Council of State, 1987).

Morales, Salvador, *Conquest and colonization of Cuba in the 16th century* (Havana: Social Sciences Publishing House, 1984).

Morrus, Emely, *Unexpected Cuba*, originally published in *New Left Review* 88 (July–August 2014) and in Spanish in *La pupila insomne*, a digital publication.

Oltuski Ozacki, Enrique, Rodríguez Llompart, Héctor And Torres-Cuevas, Eduardo, *Memorias de la Revolución*, vols. 1 and 2 (Havana: Editorial Imagen Contemporánea, 2007 and 2008).

Pichardo Viñals, Hortensia, *Documents for the History of Cuba, vol. 1* (Havana: Social Sciences Publishing House, 1971); vols, 2 and 3 (1973); vol. 4, Parts 1 and 2 (1980).

164 BIBLIOGRPAHY

_____, *On the Ten Years' War 1868–1878* (Havana, ICL, 1979).

Ramonet, Ignacio, *One Hundred Hours with Fidel* (Havana: Publications Office of the Council of State of the Republic of Cuba, 2006).

Risquet Valdés, Jorge, *Forty Years of Cuban Solidarity with Africa* (Havana: Editorial SI-MAR S.A., 1999).

_____, *The Second Front of Ché in the Congo* (Havana: Casa Editorial, April 2000).

Roa García, Raúl, *The Revolution of the 30th Went to Bolina* (Havana: Book Institute, 1969).

Rodríguez, Juan Carlos, *Girón, la batalla inevitable* (Havana: Editorial Capitán San Luis, 2005).

Rodríguez La O, Raúl, *Máximo Gómez, una vida extraordinaria* (Havana: Editora Política, 2012).

Rodríguez La O, Raúl Rodríguez, Rolando, *Cuba: The Forge of a Nation,* vol. 3 (Havana: Social Sciences Publishing House, 2005).

_____, *Dos Ríos. A Caballo y Con el Sol en la frente* (Havana: Social Sciences Publishing House, 2001).

Rojas, Marta, *The Moncada Trial* (Havana: Social Sciences Publishing House, 1988).

Roy De Leuchsenring, Emilio, *Cuba does not owe its independence to the United States* (Havana: Ediciones Tertulia, 1960; and Havana: Editora Política, 1997).

Stonor Sanders, French, *La CIA y la guerra fría* (Havana: Social Sciences Publishing House, 2003).

Torres-Cuevas, Eduardo, Loyola Vega, Oscar, *History of Cuba, 1492–1898. Formación y Liberación de la Nación* (Havana: Editorial Pueblo y Educación, 2001).

Torreira Crespo, Ramón, and Buajasán Marowi, *Operation Peter Pan: Un caso de guerra psicológica contra Cuba* (Havana: Editora Política, 2000).

Universidad Nacional Autónoma De México, *Chronology of interventions in Latin America,* vol. 2: 1849–1898.

Valdés, Jacinto-Vivanco, Dapena, *Operation Mongoose: Prelude to the Direct Invasion of Cuba* (Havana: Editorial Capitán San Luis, 2003).

Valdés Galarraga, Ramiro, *Diccionario pensamiento martiano* (Havana: Social Sciences Publishing House, 2002).

Vitier, Cintio, *International Conference José Martí, Universal Man* (Center of Martían Studies, April 1992).

Zaldívar Dieguez, Andrés, *Blockade, the Longest Economic Siege in History* (Havana: Editorial Capitán San Luis, 2003).

Zaldívar Dieguez, Andrés, and Etcheverry Vázquez, Pedro, *A Fascinating Story, the Trujillo Conspiracy* (Havana: Editorial Capitán San Luis, 2010).

Notes

1. Political and economic process initiated by Mikhail Gorbachev, General Secretary of the Communist Party of the Soviet Union, February 1985, that entailed the restructuring or the implementation of reforms of the socialist economy.

2. An international organization founded in 1949 whose main function was the coordination of the economic and social development of the socialist countries. It was formed by Albania, the German Democratic Republic (GDR), Bulgaria, Czechoslovakia, Hungary, Poland, Romania, USSR, and later joined by Vietnam and Cuba. China, the Democratic People's Republic of Korea, and Mongolia attended as observers. Ángela Ferriol and Rita Castiñeiras Therbom, *Política Social: El mundo contemporáneo y las experiencias de Cuba y Suecia* (Montevideo, Uruguay: Pontografica, 2004), 130.

3. Fidel Castro Ruz speech, July 26, 1989, in the province of Camagüey, in commemoration of the thirtieth anniversary of July 26, 1959.

4. Ibid.

5. The rectification campaign began in the second half of the 1980s and was aimed at reversing what were seen as movements toward the restoration of capitalism.

6. The Cuban Democracy Act was a bill presented by U.S. Congressman Robert Torricelli and passed in 1992. It prohibited foreign-based subsidiaries of U.S. companies from trading with Cuba, travel to Cuba by U.S. citizens, and family remittances to Cuba.

NOTES TO PAGES 31 – 58

7. The Cuban Liberty and Democratic Solidarity Act of 1996 (Helms-Burton Act) strengthened the U.S. embargo against Cuba. The act extended the territorial application of the initial embargo to apply to foreign companies trading with Cuba, and it penalized foreign companies allegedly "trafficking" in property formerly owned by U.S. citizens but confiscated by Cuba after the Revolution. The act also covers property formerly owned by Cubans who have since become U.S. citizens.

8. Organoponics is a Cuban invention. The term was coined to distinguish it from other intensive, high-yielding horticulture production systems, such as hydroponics, which grows plants in water and inert substrates enriched with mineral nutrients. Although Havana's urban farmers experimented with hydroponics, that technology depends on a reliable supply of chemical inputs.

9. Testimony of Ulises Rosales del Toro (1942), Division General, who holds the title of Hero of the Republic of Cuba. He was a member of the rebel army during the guerrilla struggle in the Sierra Maestra. After the triumph of the Revolution, he was promoted in degree and position. He became Chief of the General Staff of the Revolutionary Armed Forces.

10. Ibid.

11. A system of business management and administration that aims to maximize the efficiency and competitiveness of socialist state enterprises by giving all managers and workers powers and responsibilities, an advanced concept of business management, and initiative, creativity, and responsibility.

12. People who have enriched themselves illegally.

13. This system of food distribution establishes the amount of subsidized rations each Cuban receives and how often supplies can be obtained.

14. The centers whose debates we participated in included, among others: the Lenin Central Workshop, the Dos Ríos and República Dominicana sugar mills, the Mártires de Barbados Basic Association of Cooperative Production, the university and the port of Camagüey; the Haydée Santamaría printing company, the Camilo Cienfuegos cane cutters brigade, the Paquito Rosales School, and the Center of Genetic Engineering and Biotechnology, Santiago de Cuba.

   In Havana, the Cuban Association of Sciences, the entity of Casts and Dies, the broadcasting stations Radio Rebelde, Radio Reloj, and Radio Progreso, *Bohemia* magazine, the contingents Héroes de Playa Girón, Blas Roca Calderío, Héroes del Moncada, Frank País, Sexto Congreso, Obras de los Panamericanos, the Cuban Institute of Radio and Television, the steel entities Cubana de Acero and Antillana de Acero, the Hatuey Brewery, the Pedro Kourí Institute, the Centre for the Production of Laboratory Animals, the Ciénaga Railway Workshops, the Ñico López Refinery, the Iron Fittings

NOTES TO PAGES 64 – 68

Factory of Guanabacoa, the Calixto García Hospital and the Frank País Orthopedic Hospital, the Centre of Immunoassay, the Headquarters of the Hydraulic Resources entities, and the Port.

In the Province of Villa Clara, the Mechanical Plant; the Industry of Production of Household Goods, INPUD; the Efraín Alfonso Sugar Mill, the Port of Caibarién; and the Campaña de Las Villas Contingent, of Santa María Cay.

In the Province of Holguín, the Factory of Combined Harvesters Revolución de Octubre, the Factory of Farming Equipment 26 de Julio, Pedro Soto Alba Enterprise, the Batteries Factory, the Onel Cañete Shoe Factory, and the Revolución de Octubre Brigade of Cane Cutters.

In the Province of Cienfuegos, the Stones Mill El Purio, the Lenin Contingent, the Electronuclear Enterprise, the Pepito Tey Sugar Mill, the Carlos Manuel de Céspedes Thermoelectric Factory, and the Citrus Enterprise Ceiba y Ceballos. In the Province of Guantánamo, the Emilio Daudinot Contingent of the Caujerí Valley, the Coffee Roasting Mill, the Chocolate Factory of Baracoa, the Enterprise of Maritime Works, and the Eduardo Delgado Contingent.

Also, the University, the Children's Hospital and the Livestock Enterprise of the Province of Pinar del Río; the Juan de Mata Reyes Cigarette Factory, in Trinidad, Province of Sancti Spíritus; the Causeway and El Vaquerito Contingent of Cayo Coco, Province of Ciego de Ávila; the UNECA Contingent of Varadero, in the Province of Matanzas; the Cauto Dam and the Dairy Complex of Bayamo, in the Province of Granma; and the cigar factories José Martí, Carlos Baliño, Partagás, Rey del Mundo, and La Corona, among others.

15. *Marabú i*s the Cuban name for sicklebush, a prickly, invasive weed that blights agriculture. Harvested and processed into charcoal, it became a profitable export item in the twenty-first century.

16. Ignacio Agramonte y Loynáz (1841–1873) was a Cuban revolutionary who played an important part in the Ten-Year War (1868–1878), the first of three wars that Cuba fought against Spain for its independence.

17. On December 15, 1895, Cuban rebels engaged Spanish troops near the town of Cruces in the fields of the Mal Tiempo (Bad Weather) sugar mill, setting fire to the sugarcane and attacking the Spanish with machetes.

18. Construction of the Juragua nuclear power plant was suspended in 1992 after the collapse of the Soviet Union and the termination of Soviet economic aid to Cuba.

19. A town in the province of Matanzas that is one of the largest resorts in the Caribbean.

20. Blas Roca Calderio was a Marxist theorist who served as president of the National Assembly of People's Power in Cuba from 1976 to 1981 (he died

168   NOTES TO PAGES 87 – 94

in 1987). He was also head of the Communist Party of Cuba before the Revolution.

21. The U.S. political scientist Francis Fukuyama coined this term in his 1992 book, *The End of History and the Last Man* (New York: Free Press, 1992).

22. The term "Washington Consensus" refers to the economic policies imposed by the International Monetary Fund (IMF), the World Bank, and the U.S. Department of the Treasury. The consensus was based on neoliberal ideology about the "free market" and government intervention in the economies of the Global South. The market purportedly fostered economic development, whereas state intervention hindered it.

23. The Free Trade Area of the Americas (FTAA) was a proposed agreement to eliminate or reduce trade barriers among countries in the Americas, excluding Cuba. Negotiations to establish the FTAA failed when all parties failed to reach an agreement by the 2005 deadline they had set for themselves.

24. U.S. minister, social activist, and human rights advocate. In 1967, he founded the Interreligious Foundation for Community Organization (IFCO). He was Deputy General Secretary of the National Council of Churches from 1973 to 1978, when he returned to IFCO as its co-executive manager. In 1992, he founded Friendship Caravans of Pastors for Peace to offer humanitarian aid to countries that needed it. He brought to Cuba computing equipment, buses, medicines, and school materials, without asking for authorization from the U.S. government, because he intended to break the blockade of Cuba. He died in September 2010, and was buried in Cuba, in accordance with his will.

25. The United States Military Government in Cuba (1898–1902), the Second Occupation of Cuba (1906–09), the Sugar Intervention (1917–1922).

26. Fernando Ortiz Fernández (1881–1969), an expert in anthropology, archaeology, and ethnology. Also a lawyer and journalist, he made important contributions to the research of Cuban culture and its African roots and to the historical formation of the Cuban nation. His works have been translated into other languages.

27. This refers to the control over land and Indians granted by the Spanish colonizers. It entailed the distribution of groups of Indians to each Spanish settler, called an *encomendero* (master), and that meant the subjugation of the aborigines to the servitude regime. It entailed a ruthless and cruel exploitation of the indigenous population.

28. José Antonio Aponte y Ulabarra. Black Creole, freeman, and carpenter, also known for his sculpture and painting.

29. An unproven conspiracy named after the stairway where slaves accused of crimes were whipped until they confessed, or died.

30. Gabriel de la Concepción Valdés (1809–1844) is considered the most

NOTES TO PAGES 95 – 99   169

popular Cuban poet the nineteenth century. Of mixed-race background in a slave society, he suffered discrimination and prejudice.

31. Máximo Gómez Báez (1836–1905), General of the Liberation Army in the Guerra de los Diez Años (the Ten-Year War), and General in Chief of the Cuban revolutionary troops in the War of 1895. He was born in Santo Domingo, Dominican Republic. He settled in Cuba in 1866 and enlisted in the fight for Cuban independence in October 14, 1868. He died in Havana on June 17, 1905.

32. Ignacio Agramonte y Loynaz (1841–1873), lawyer. For his merit in the pro-independence war against Spain, he reached the rank of General Major of the Liberation Army. He was known as "The Major." One of the greatest leaders of the Ten-Year War, he organized the renowned Cavalry of Camagüey, which achieved great victories against the Spanish colonialist troops. He died in combat May 11, 1873, at thirty-two years of age.

33. Cintio Vitier (1921–2009), novelist, essayist, and critic. Born in the United States, he renounced his U.S. citizenship in 1958. One of the most important Cuban writers of all time, with an extensive body of work comprising poetry, essays, narrative, criticism, and translations. A great admirer of the work of José Martí.

34. Ricardo Alarcón de Quesada, former president of the National Assembly of People's Power, in the February 24, 1995, session.

35. Calixto García Íñiguez joined the Ten-Year War on October 13, 1868. An autodidact, he had solid military training. He participated in the Storming of Bayamo and in its ultimate defense. In August 1869, he was designated Chief of the General Staff of Máximo Gómez. During the war, he participated in several battles and led important operations of the troops under his command. He was promoted several times until he achieved the rank of General Major, in 1872. On September 6, 1874, the enemy managed to surround him. He preferred to die rather than be captured by the Spaniards, and he shot himself. Seriously injured, he was captured and imprisoned in Spain. As result of the Pact of Zanjón, he was released on May 29, 1878. He moved to New York, with the intention to prepare a new war.

36. José Martí, *Obras Completas*, vol. 1 (Havana: Social Sciences Publishing House, 1975), 212.

37. Its Grounds and Statutes were approved by the Cuban Patriotic League of Tampa, United States of America, on January 8, 1892. The creation of the party took place a few months later, on April 10.

38. José Martí, *Obras Completas*, vol. 4, 93–101.

39. Flor Crombet Tejera (1851–1895) joined the Liberation Army in November 1868. He was promoted to different military ranks until achieving the rank of brigadier. He took part in the Protest of Baraguá. He worked in the preparations of the *Guerra Chiquita* (Small War), and for it, he was detained

170   NOTES TO PAGES 99 – 108

and sent to Spain. After twenty-three months in prison, he managed to escape and fled to Central America. On April 1, 1895, he arrived, along with Antonio Maceo and other patriots, to join the war for independence. He died in combat a few days later (April 10). He was posthumously awarded the rank of general major.

40. José Martí, *Obras Completas*, vol. 19, 229.

41. Rolando Rodríguez, *Dos Ríos: A caballo y con el sol en la frente* (Havana: Social Sciences Publishing House, 2001), 63.

42. José Martí, *Obras Completas*, vol. 16, 98.

43. Aníbal Escalante Beatón and Calixto García, *Su campaña en el 95* (Havana: Social Sciences Publishing House, 1978), in "Memoria escrita y visual de la Guerra Hispano-Cubana-Norteamericana," 1898, by Nydia Sarabia, historian, journalist, and essayist, https://studylib.es/doc/7006715/memoria-escrita-y-visual-de-la-guerra-hispano.

44. Political organization founded in 1908 by Evaristo Estenoz Corominas, a veteran of the Liberation Army, to oppose the racist treatment of Black and mixed-race Cubans that was a legacy of centuries of slavery. The party consisted almost entirely of formerly enslaved Black men.

45. Rubén Martínez Villena (1899–1934). Cuban revolutionary and one of the most important intellectuals of his generation. Leader of the Communist Party of Cuba, which he joined in 1927. Main ideological architect of the popular struggle that overthrew the dictator Gerardo Machado. He had a brief but productive career in literature.

46. Gerardo Lorenzo Machado Morales (1869–1939). Fifth president of the Republic of Cuba. He joined the Liberation Army while still very young, attaining the rank of brigadier. He occupied important positions in the army and became President of the Republic May 20, 1925.

47. Alfredo López Arencibia (1894–1926). Typographic worker. Outstanding trade union leader, organizer, and tenacious fighter for the unity of the working class. He understood early on the need to organize workers in an independent and unitary class organization to fight for its demands. He was founder and leader of Federación Obrera de La Habana (the Labor Federation of Havana) (1921) and afterward, CNOC. He stood out for his moral values and his firm and incorruptible attitude. He was arrested during Machado's dictatorship, tortured, and then murdered July 20, 1926.

48. Carlos Benigno Baliño y López (1848–1926). Pioneer of Cuban Marxist thought. He immigrated to the United States in late 1868 or 1869 for economic reasons. There, he was a tobacco worker in Florida. In Key West, he edited the newspaper *La Tribuna del Pueblo*, which promoted the freedom of Cuba and its working class. He met José Martí and in 1892 endorsed the Memorandum of Association of the Cuban Revolutionary Party, founded by Martí. At the end of the war against Spain, he returned to

NOTES TO PAGES 108 – 110   171

Cuba, where he continued his political activity in several organizations and collaborated with different publications. He died June 18, 1926.

49. This organization was reconstituted in 1930 to overthrow the Machado dictatorship.

50. President of the United States from 1933 to April 12, 1945. He died before finishing his term.

51. Carlos Manuel de Céspedes y Quesada, Cuban politician, diplomat and intellectual. Son of Carlos Manuel de Céspedes. He achieved the rank of colonel in the War of 1895. During the Republic, he served as a House Representative. He performed diplomatic functions in several countries and was State Secretary of President Alfredo Zayas.

52. Sergio Carbó y Morera, journalist; Porfirio Franca y Álvarez de la Campa, attorney, banker and economist; Ramón Grau San Martín, faculty, University of Havana School of Medicine; José Miguel Irisarri y Gamio, attorney; and Guillermo Portela y Möller, faculty, University of Havana School of Law.

53. Antonio Guiteras Holmes (1906–1935). A member of the University Student Directorate, he opposed the Machado dictatorship. He founded the Revolutionary Union. He rejected the mediation of Sumner Welles and planned an assault on the Bayamo fortress and then withdrew his forces; he would go to the Sierra Maestra to launch the armed struggle. He was delegate of the Pentarchy government in Oriente province. During the One-Hundred-Day government, he was Secretary of Government, War, and the Marine. He exerted great influence in that government and fostered most of the revolutionary and popular measures it adopted. After the overthrow of the One-Hundred-Day government, he decided to organize an armed insurrection and founded Young Cuba. He had a secret plan: to organize an expedition from Mexico that would disembark in the east and march to the Sierra Maestra. Batista, chief of the army, offered him a position in the government if he abandoned his insurrectionary plans but he refused. He was planning to leave for a May 7, 1935, expedition from El Morrillo, Matanzas province, but he was betrayed. He died in combat.

54. Eduardo René Chibás (1907–1951). He was prominent in the fight against the Machado dictatorship and denounced the corruption of the period. He was a member of the University Student Directory. He was expelled from the university because of his opposition to the prorogation of powers imposed by Gerardo Machado. He was influential in the One-Hundred-Day government. He joined the Authentic Party but was disillusioned by its corruption. In 1947, he founded the Orthodox Party under the slogan "Decency versus Money."

55. Carlos Prío Socarrás (1903–1977). He began his political activity at the University of Havana against Gerardo Machado. He was secretary of the University Student Directory in 1930.

172   NOTES TO PAGE 112

56. Lázaro Peña González (1911–1974). Cuban trade union leader. He joined
     the Communist Party of Cuba in 1929. He was General Secretary of the
     Tobacco Trade Union and a member of the Executive Committee of the
     National Labor Confederation of Cuba, which he led from 1935. He suffered
     imprisonment and torture. In 1939, he was elected General Secretary of the
     Confederation of Workers of Cuba (CTC) and delegate of the Constituent
     Assembly of 1940. He was among the founders of the Confederation of
     Workers of Latin America (CTAL) and the World Trade Union Federation
     (FSM). He faced up against imperialism and the authentic governments
     that, from 1947, forced the division of the Cuban labor movement and
     imposed Eusebio Mujal's appointment in the direction of the CTC. The
     dictatorship of Fulgencio Batista did not allow his entry to the country at
     his return from the Third Congress of FSM, celebrated in Vienna, October
     1953. After the revolutionary triumph, he joined in the reconstruction of
     the trade union movement. In 1961, at the Eleventh Congress of the CTC,
     he was elected General Secretary, a post he held until 1966. He was a
     member of the Central Committee of the Communist Party of Cuba since its
     constitution in 1965. With his health seriously affected, he worked intensely
     in the preparation and organization of the Thirteenth Congress of the CTC,
     in November 1973. He died May 11, 1974.
57. Jesús Menéndez Larrondo (1911–1948), leader of the Cuban sugar workers,
     Communist militant. In 1932, he founded the National Labor Union of the
     Sugar Industry. Founder, along with Lázaro Peña, of the CTC, in 1939. He
     was delegate to the Constituent Assembly that year and was elected House
     Representative by the Communist Revolutionary Union Party in 1940. He
     was murdered by a captain of the Rural Guard in the Manzanillo railway on
     January 22, 1948.
58. Aracelio Iglesias Díaz (1901–1948), Communist militant and trade
     union leader of the Cuban port workers. In 1938, he was elected General
     Secretary of the Trade Union of Stevedores and Day Laborers. He joined
     the Executive Committee of the CTC upon its creation. In 1946, he held
     the office of secretary of the Local Maritime Labor Federation of the Port
     of Havana. He obtained important achievements for the workers. He was
     murdered October 17, 1948.
59. José María Pérez Capote (1911–1957), Cuban trade union leader of the
     transport sector, member of the Communist Party. He participated in
     manifestations against the dictatorship of Gerardo Machado and in other
     actions. In 1935, he founded the first trade union in the transport sector,
     and the following year, he became General Secretary of Allied Employees
     and Workers of Buses. In 1938, he led the foundation of the Federation
     of Workers of the Province of Havana, and in 1939 he participated in the
     drafting of the constitution of the Confederation of Workers of Cuba. He

NOTES TO PAGES 112 – 119   173

was elected substitute to the Constituent Assembly of 1940 and later, House Representative. He opposed the division of the labor movement in 1947 promoted by trade union gangsters protected by the government. He fought the dictatorship of Fulgencio Batista and was arrested on several occasions. On November 20, 1957, he was kidnapped, tortured, and murdered.

60. Federico Laredo Brú (1875–1946). A member of the Liberation Army, he achieved the rank of colonel. After the establishment of the Republic, he occupied several positions in different governments until he gained the presidency of the Republic from 1936 to 1940. Later, he was appointed Minister of Justice during the Batista dictatorship (from 1940 to 1944).

61. Ricardo Alarcón de Quesada, "La Constitución de 1940 en nuestra historia," closing session of the Ninth National Meeting of the Cuban Society of Constitutional and Administrative Law, published October 9, 2010.

62. Pejorative expression for workers' leaders who sold out to employers and whose corrupt and demagogic elements were represented by Eusebio Mujal Barniol (1915–1985), who betrayed and renounced the Marxist ideals of his youth and returned to retrograde positions, becoming a militant anti-communist. He usurped the management of the CTC in 1947 and expelled communist trade union leaders. "Mujalism" instituted an obligatory trade union quota that became a source of fraud and personal enrichment. He established trade unions of a gangster nature, like those that existed in the United States at that time.

63. Katiuska Blanco Castiñeira, *Fidel Castro Ruz, Guerrillero del Tiempo*, vol. 2 (Havana: Ediciones Abril, 2011), 5–14.

64. Rubén Batista Rubio (1931–1953). First student martyr in the struggle against the Batista dictatorship.

65. Museum with preserved remainders of a stone quarry where, under Spanish colonialism, prisoners were condemned to hard labor. In April 1870, José Martí, barely a teenager, was confined in this place and was forced to work up to twelve hours a day, under inhumane conditions, with a shackle attached to his right leg and chained to his waist.

66. Abel Santamaría Cuadrado (1927–1953), militant of the Orthodox Youth, later a leader of the movement founded by Fidel Castro, and second chief of the assault on the Moncada Fortress. He was arrested, tortured, and murdered July 26, 1953.

67. Ramiro Valdés Menéndez (1932–). After the events of July 26, 1953, he was imprisoned in Isla de Pinos until May 15, 1955. Upon the granting of amnesty because of popular pressure, he left for Mexico. He took part in the expedition of the *Granma* and integrated the guerrilla nucleus that initiated the fight in Sierra Maestra. He was the second chief of the invading column of Ejército Rebelde (the Rebel Army), led by Ernesto "Che" Guevara. With

174 NOTES TO PAGES 119 – 120

the triumph of the Revolution on January 1, 1959, he held the rank of major. He was Home Secretary from 1961 to 1968 and from 1979 to 1985. He was appointed Minister of Informatics and Communications from 2005 to 2010. Currently, he is a member of the Politburo of the Communist Party of Cuba and vice president of the Councils of State and of Ministers. He is a deputy in the National Assembly of People's Power and a Hero of the Republic of Cuba.

68. Jesús Montané Oropesa (1923–1999). One of the leaders of the movement founded by Fidel Castro. He participated in the assault on the Moncada Fortress and was detained and imprisoned. He left prison on May 15, 1955, and joined the National Directorate of the July 26 Movement. He took part in the *Granma* expedition, but he was captured after disembarking and imprisoned until January 1, 1959. From 1973 until his death at the age of seventy-six, he worked as Fidel Castro's assistant.

69. Renato Guitart Rosell (1930–1953). Joined Fidel Castro's movement. He was one of the few who knew the details of the Moncada Fortress assault during its planning. Along with Abel Santamaría, he leased the premises that would be used as lodging for the combatants in Santiago de Cuba. He developed the plan for the Moncada assault and provided information about weapons and assets. He led the taking of the control station No. 3. He entered the fortress and was mortally wounded in the exchange of gunfire.

70. Pedro Manuel Sarría Tartabull (1900–1972), Cuban career officer. He joined the Cuban army in 1925 and attained the rank of lieutenant. After the Moncada assault, he surprised Fidel and his companions Oscar Alcalde and José Suárez at dawn on August 1, 1953, and prevented their assassination. For that, he was discharged from the army. After the Revolution succeeded, he was promoted to captain by Fidel himself.

71. Haydée Santamaría Cuadrado (1923–1980). One of two women who participated in the assault on the Moncada Fortress. She was sent to prison. After her release on February 20, 1954, she joined the National Directorate of the July 26 Movement. She also helped compile and organize the notes that Fidel managed to take out of prison, written with lemon juice. The notes would be reconstructed for his speech in the Moncada trial, the oration that would come to be known as "La historia me absolverá" (History will absolve me). She supported the guerrilla forces in Sierra Maestra under the direction of Fidel, who entrusted her with obtaining funds and weapons, and the assembling of revolutionaries who were abroad. She returned to Cuba when the Revolution triumphed and worked in the Ministry of Education. Later, she founded and directed for many years Casa de las Américas (House of the Americas). She is a Heroine of the Cuban Revolution.

NOTES TO PAGES 122 – 124 175

72. Melba Hernández Rodríguez del Rey (1921–2014) was detained and imprisoned for her participation in the July 26 taking of the Saturnino Lora Civil Hospital in Santiago de Cuba. After being released from prison, she, with Lidia Castro and Haydée Santamaría, compiled and organized the notes that Fidel used in his speech in the Moncada trial. She also helped prepare the *Granma* expedition. Afterward, she joined the Ejército Rebelde (the Rebel Army); she is a Heroine of the Cuban Revolution.

73. Jacobo Arbenz Guzmán (1913–1971), president of Guatemala from 1951 to 1954. During his presidency, he implemented agrarian reform to provide poor peasants with land. He carried out a program of road and railway construction that broke the monopoly of U.S. subsidiary companies. He initiated a process to secure the rights of the native peoples. In 1954, he expropriated land held by the United Fruit Company and established a modest tax on the export of bananas to finance social programs. He was overthrown in a coup d'état and resigned on June 27, 1954, with the intention to stop the armed aggression initiated ten days before from Honduran territory by a paramilitary group supported by the United States, which, through the CIA, organized his overthrow.

74. Ignacio Ramonet, *Cien horas con Fidel* (Havana: Oficina de Publicaciones del Consejo de Estado, 2006), 197.

75. Jorge Ricardo Masetti, *Los que luchan y los que lloran* (Havana: Editorial Madiedo, 1960). Notes of the Cuban editor to *Cien horas con Fidel*, 712.

76. Frank País García (1934–1957), one of the leaders of the fight against the Batista dictatorship.

77. Rafael García Bárcena (1907–1961) participated in the struggles against the Machado dictatorship (1925–1933). In 1938, he graduated as Doctor in Philosophy and Writing and worked as a journalist during the 1940s. He helped found the Orthodox Party in 1947 but left it in 1948. In May 1952, he founded the National Revolutionary Movement, backed by students, and he instigated a civic-military conspiracy to overthrow the dictatorship. When it was quashed in April 1953, he was tried and sentenced to prison. He later went into exile. In February 1959, he was appointed Cuba's ambassador to Brazil, a position he held until mid-1961.

78. Flavio Bravo Pardo (1921–1988) led Juventud Socialista (Socialist Youth) for twelve years from its inception in 1944. He was vice president of the World Federation of Democratic Youth. He integrated the Central Committee of the Popular Socialist Party (PSP). He was persecuted and was arrested several times. Before the March 10, 1952, coup d'état, he led numerous acts of protest. In1953, he was among the leaders of the Communist Party who had to go underground. After the Revolution, he had important assignments in the Revolutionary Armed Forces, in the National Directorate of the Integrated Revolutionary Organizations (ORI), and, later,

176 NOTES TO PAGES 125 – 127

the Partido Unido de la Revolución Socialista de Cuba (United Party of the Socialist Revolution of Cuba/PURSC). He served in Algeria and Guinea, in 1963 and 1967, in international missions. He was a member of the Council of State, vice president of the Council of Ministers, and from 1981 until his death, president of the National Assembly of People's Power.

79. Otto Parellada Echeverría (1928–1956). In December 1950, he traveled to the United States for work, first in Miami and then in New York. After the March 10, 1952, coup d'état, he returned to Cuba and joined the fight against the Batista dictatorship.

80. Tony Alomá Serrano (1927–1956). After the Moncada fortress assault, he joined the clandestine fight against the Batista dictatorship.

81. José Tey Saint Blancard (1932–1956) was a prominent student leader at the Training College for Teachers of the East. Along with Frank País, as president, he joined the first revolutionary organizations against the Batista dictatorship and helped found the July 26 Movement in Santiago de Cuba. He was president of the Eastern University Student Federation.

82. Celia Sánchez Manduley (1920–1980), Heroine of the Cuban Revolution. She participated in the July 26 Movement. Under her war name, Norma, she became a legendary figure in the *Granma* expedition and the beginning of the guerrilla war in the Sierra Maestra. She was the first woman combatant in the Rebel Army.

83. Fructuoso Rodríguez (1933–1957) led protests against the March 10, 1952, coup d'état. He was the second national leader of the Revolutionary Student Movement, after José Antonio Echeverría. He assumed the leadership of the Revolutionary Directorate upon the death of José Antonio. He worked in its reorganization, in establishing responsibilities and disciplinary measures, in defining new tactics, in the consignment of recovered weapons to Sierra Maestra, in the creation of a guerrilla front in Las Villas, in the designation of Faure Chomón, Chief of Action of the Directory. He left the country clandestinely to prepare and launch an armed expedition.

84. Juan Pedro Carbó Serviá (1926–1957), student leader who opposed Batista's coup d'état of March 10, 1952. He was prominent in student actions and demonstrations against the regime. He was part of the Revolutionary Directorate since its founding. With José Antonio Echeverría, he was in the interview with Fidel in Mexico in August 1955, where the Letter of Mexico was signed. He carried out the mission of executing Colonel Blanco Rico, chief of the Military Intelligence Service.

85. José Machado Rodríguez, "Machadito" (1932–1957), member of the Revolutionary Directorate. Upon Batista's coup d'état, he joined the fight against the tyrant. He was in the first ranks of the student demonstrations and was one of the closest collaborators of José Antonio Echeverría.

86. José Westbrook Rosales (1937–1957), member of the Revolutionary

NOTES TO PAGES 127 – 128 177

Directorate, opposed the dictatorship of Fulgencio Batista. He joined the conspiracy led by the university professor Rafael García Bárcena to assault the Military City of Columbia, an action that was thwarted. At the university, he intensified his relations with revolutionary students. He participated in the meeting between José Antonio Echeverría and Fidel Castro in Mexico where the Letter of Mexico was signed.

87. Located in the Municipality of Guamá, in the southern part of Santiago de Cuba.

88. Raúl Pujol Arencibia (1918–1957), revolutionary combatant. After the Moncada assault, he joined the clandestine activities against the dictatorship. He was one of the organizers of the movement of Civic Resistance in Santiago de Cuba and his house was a meeting place of the July 26 Movement.

89. Participant in the Moncada fortress assault. He was imprisoned in Isla de Pinos. Once he was released, he went to Mexico and joined the *Granma* expedition. A Commander of the Revolution, he had important responsibilities.

90. Crescencio Pérez Montano (1895–1985), Commander of the Rebel Army. One of the leaders of the group organized by Celia Sánchez in the eastern mountains to assist the *Granma* expedition. After the defeat of Alegría de Pío, he joined the rebel forces as a combatant.

91. Camilo Cienfuegos Gorriarán (1932–1959), member of the *Granma* expedition. In the Sierra Maestra he joined the José Martí Column No. 1, led by Fidel Castro. He quickly demonstrated his astuteness as a guerrilla leader. He was appointed to lead the Antonio Maceo Column No. 2, which, along with the forces led by Ernesto "Che" Guevara, in August 1958 led a campaign in the center of the country. Once the revolutionary government was established, he was designated Chief of the General Staff of the Rebel Army. Upon the betrayal of Hubert Matos, who was managing the Camagüey province, Cienfuegos went there and occupied the fortress where Matos was, and without firing one bullet, arrested him for high treason. On October 28, he made a work-related trip to Camagüey and on his return trip the same day, his airplane disappeared. An intensive search was carried out but Cienfuegos was never found. He was a legendary figure, known as the Hero of Yaguajay.

92. Eloy Gutiérrez Menoyo (Madrid, Spain, 1934–Havana, Cuba, 2012) joined the armed struggle against Batista after the death of his brother, Carlos, taking part in the March 13, 1957, assault on the presidential palace. He was Chief of Action of the Revolutionary Directorate in Havana and in charge of organizing the guerrilla front in the zone of Escambray in Las Villas. In November 1957, he proclaimed the opening of the Second National Front. In July 1958, he refused to hand over his command. There was division inside the Revolutionary Directorate and he was expelled from

the organization. He retreated to the southern mountains accompanied by his men and remained there until the end of the war. Beginning in early 1959, he expressed his disagreement with the revolutionary process and in January 1961 fled the country in a vessel to the United States, where he was arrested and held for six months and then released. He joined the terrorist organization Alpha 66 and was appointed its military director. In December 1964, he led the disembarkation near Baracoa and a few days later was arrested and sentenced to thirty years' imprisonment. He was released before completing his sentence. He traveled to Spain and then to the United States, where he founded Cambio Cubano (Cuban Change). He later traveled to Cuba and met with Fidel Castro and in 2003 settled permanently in Havana, where he died in 2012.

93. Félix Torres (1917–2008), Secretary of the Peasants' Front of the Popular Socialist Party.

94. Faustino Pérez (1920–1992) joined the First National Directorate of the July 26 Movement. He was a member of the *Granma* expedition. Fidel Castro designated him as a delegate of the July 26 Movement in Havana. After the failure of the April 9, 1958, strike, he joined the guerrilla fight.

95. José Cantón Navarro, *Cuba, el desafío del yugo y la estrella* (Havana: Editorial SI-MAR S.A., 1996) 196.

96. See Enzo Infante, "La reunión de Alto de Mompié," in Enrique Oltuski, Héctor Rodríguez Llompart y Eduardo Torres Cuevas, eds., *Memorias de la Revolución* (Havana: Ediciones Imagen Contemporánea, 2007).

97. Amels Escalante Colás and Juan Sánchez Rodríguez, *Un triunfo decisivo* (Havana: Casa Editorial Verde Olivo, 2006), 23.

98. Eulogio Cantillo Porras (1911–1978), career soldier. At the time of the March 10, 1952, coup d'état , he was chief of the air force. He did not participate in the coup but accepted it and was promoted. He was appointed chief of the Joint General Staff and acted as chief of operations of the army in Oriente.

99. Carlos Manuel Piedra Piedra, Cuban lawyer. The oldest Supreme Court justice when Fulgencio Batista fled Cuba January 1, 1959. He was summoned by General Eulogio Cantillo to lead a civic-military junta as president of the Republic. He accepted but there was no one willing to swear him in so he never held the presidency.

100. Manuel Urrutia Lleó, President of the Republic of Cuba from January to July 1959. A lawyer, he was magistrate of the Court of Santiago de Cuba from 1949 to 1957. On March 14, 1957, in his capacity as president of the Criminal Division of the Eastern Court, he voted to absolve the revolutionaries who were on trial for the November 30 uprising in Santiago de Cuba, along with the members of the *Granma* expedition. In the trial, he legitimized armed opposition to Batista's government, an unconstitutional

NOTES TO PAGES 133 – 142 179

regime that had been established through a coup d'état. In recognition of his position, the Directorate of the July 26 Movement proposed him for the provisional presidency of the Republic.

101. Ramón Barquín López, Cuban military officer. He conspired in April 1956 against Fulgencio Batista in the so-called Conspiración de los Puros (Conspiracy of the Cigars) with a group of other soldiers. After the conspiracy was discovered, he was sentenced to eight years in prison. He was released January 1, 1959. After Batista fled, Eulogio Cantillo appointed Barquin as Chief of the General Staff of the army but the revolutionary government did not keep him in that position. Opposed to the Revolution's radicalism, he deserted his position as military attaché in Spain and went into exile in the United States. He settled initially in Miami where he established links with counterrevolutionary organizations. Afterward, he resided in Puerto Rico, where he died on March 3, 2008.

102. "Covert Action Program Against the Castro Regime," https://history.state.gov/historicaldocuments/frus1958-60v06/d481.

103. Ibid.

104. Operation Peter Pan, a clandestine subversion campaign (December 26, 1960, to October 23, 1962) involving the U.S. State Department; representatives of the Catholic Church in Miami and Cuba; the Central Intelligence Agency; and various counterrevolutionary organizations. It promoted what supposedly was a spontaneous migratory process. More than 14,000 Cuban children left for the United States without their parents, who, in many cases, never saw them again.

105. Municipality east of the Artemisa province that at that time was part of the province of Havana.

106. Military camp that had been the first military fortress of the Batista regime, located in the municipality of Marianao. On September 14, 1959, it was turned into a school and renamed Ciudad Libertad (Freedom City).

107. Use of lands owned by someone else.

108. In Pedro Etcheverry Vázquez and Santiago Gutiérrez Oceguera, *Bandidismo, derrota de la CIA* (Havana: Editorial Capitán San Luis, 2008).

109. The Monroe Doctrine, elaborated by U.S. president James Monroe in 1823. The policy declared that the United States would not tolerate any interference by European nations in the Americas.

110. Ignacio Ramonet, *Cien horas con Fidel*, 2nd ed. (Havana: Oficina de Publicaciones del Consejo de Estado, 2006,), 307–29.

111. Letter read by Fidel Castro October 3, 1965, on the occasion of the constitution of the First Central Committee of Cuba's Communist Party.

112. José A. Cantón and Arnaldo Silva León, *Historia de Cuba 1959–1999, liberación nacional y socialismo* (Havana: Editorial Pueblo y Educación, 2009).

180 NOTES TO PAGES 144 – 148

113. Testimony of Jorge Lezcano Pérez, First Secretary of the Provincial Committee of the Party, 1985–1994.

114. "Cuba sends 'white coat army' of doctors to fight coronavirus in different countries," https://www.nbcnews.com/news/latino/cuba-sends-white-coat-army-doctors-fight-coronavirus-different-countries-n1240028.

115. The policy of racial segregation and of territorial organization that was applied in a systematic manner in South Africa until 1990.

116. On July 3, 1962, Algeria won its independence from France. On September 26, Ahmed Ben Bella was elected prime minister. On October 1, mechanized units of Morocco made an incursion in Algerian territory. Algeria's troops responded, but after a false withdrawal, Morocco counterattacked, demonstrating its military superiority. President Ben Bella asked Cuba for help. The arrival of the Cuban troops changed the correlation of the forces, which, along with the international condemnation of the invasion, led the Moroccan monarchy to make peace with Algeria on October 30, 1963.

117. Region occupied by Israel as result of the Six-Day War against neighboring countries in 1967, which resulted in the illegal occupations of the West Bank, East Jerusalem, the Sinai Peninsula, and Syria's Golan Heights.

118. Patrice Lumumba (1925–1961) founded in 1958 the National Congolese Movement (MNC), which, in alliance with other progressive forces, won the elections of May 1960. Lumumba became prime minister in a coalition government with Joseph Kasavubu, as president. The independent Democratic Republic of Congo was proclaimed July 1, 1960. Lumumba was assassinated January 17, 1961.

119. A lake in Central Africa bordering four countries: to the north, Burundi; to the west, the Democratic Republic of Congo; to the east, Tanzania; and to the south, Zambia.

120. Mobuto Sese Seko (1930–1997), Chief of the Armed Forces of Congo (formerly the Belgian Congo) after independence. He proclaimed himself president of Congo in 1965 in a coup d'état. He remained in power until his overthrow in 1997. He led one of the most violent, corrupt, and dictatorial African regimes.

121. Amílcar Cabral (1923–1973), General Secretary of the African Party for the Independence of Guinea and Cape Verde (PAIGC), which he organized in 1956. He fought the Portuguese colonial regime for his country's independence. He was assassinated January 20, 1973, when victory was imminent. In his revolutionary work, he brought together people from different ethnic groups and religious beliefs to fight for independence.

CPSIA information can be obtained
at www.ICGtesting.com
Printed in the USA
JSHW031642191122
33504JS00003B/5